Frances Gulick Jewett, Society Congregational Publishing

Luther Halsey Gulick, missionary in Hawaii, Micronesia, Japan, and China

Frances Gulick Jewett, Society Congregational Publishing

Luther Halsey Gulick, missionary in Hawaii, Micronesia, Japan, and China

ISBN/EAN: 9783337127121

Printed in Europe, USA, Canada, Australia, Japan

Cover: Foto ©ninafisch / pixelio.de

More available books at **www.hansebooks.com**

Luther Halsey Gulick

LUTHER HALSEY GULICK

MISSIONARY IN

HAWAII, MICRONESIA, JAPAN, AND CHINA

BY

FRANCES GULICK JEWETT

BOSTON AND CHICAGO
Congregational Sunday-School and Publishing Society

COPYRIGHT, 1895,
BY CONGREGATIONAL SUNDAY-SCHOOL AND PUBLISHING SOCIETY

INTRODUCTION.

IT gives me great pleasure to commend a volume which sets forth in such fitting terms the life and work of Dr. Gulick. The volume has been prepared as a labor of love by his daughter, Mrs. Jewett, than whom no one of my acquaintance is better fitted for the task, both through her thorough acquaintance with the incidents of his life and work and because of her command of language and of a style well fitted for this object. Few men have had a more varied experience on mission ground than Dr. Gulick; few have shown greater ability and power of adaptation to the most varied circumstances, and it is fitting that the record of his career in Micronesia, in the Sandwich Islands, in Spain, and in Italy should be commemorated as a part of the missionary history of the past generation.

The more I reflect upon it the more I wonder at the work which Dr. Gulick was enabled to do at Ponape, at Ebon, as Secretary of the Hawaiian Board, and, later, in the organization of missions in Papal Lands, and, last of all, in the splendid work of distributing the Scriptures in Japan and China. Certainly he must rank among the great missionaries of the world. Many in this country remember his rare eloquence in setting forth the missionary work. He has a record unsurpassed in missionary annals.

N. G. CLARK.

I will claim the whole heathen world as my countrymen.

LUTHER HALSEY GULICK.
(*Age fifteen.*)

PREFACE.

FROM the age of twelve until he was married at twenty-three Dr. Gulick was quite deprived of intimate friendship. A certain sort of compensation came, however, in the unreserved expression of himself to himself through his diligent pen and his daily journal. As a result, this journal pictures in a remarkable way the development of the soul of a conscientious child.

For this reason, and also because the larger interest centers always in what a man is and in what he is becoming rather than in what he does, the earlier years of Dr. Gulick's life in America, and the succeeding years of his growth in Micronesia, have been allowed to occupy more space in this brief history than would otherwise have been given to them. His later missionary experiences were in line with what the Christian Church already well understands. They have, therefore, been crowded into narrower compass.

In the preparation of any biography, the ideal method is that of simple compilation from letters and other manuscript. But this course has its disadvantage; for to present a character clearly in this way necessitates, as a rule, a history in two or three volumes. When that which is more brief is desired, as in the present case, there is, therefore, no alternative but to quote such part alone of what was written as, it may be hoped, will afford both help and inspiration to the reader, giving the rest in condensed narrative form.

The story of this life has been written with this thought in mind.

When these chapters have been read, it may perhaps be asked whether there were no other side to the character which has been pictured. The answer to the query is that every human life has its stronger and its weaker side, but that a daughter writes this history; and though she has striven to be honest, her father is its hero.

For the manuscript examined, I am indebted to the kindness of many friends and to the courtesy of the officers of the American Board who have permitted free access to all that is on file in their rooms in Boston.

Personally my obligation is greatest to the close circle of family relatives without whose earnest coöperation and encouragement this work would not have been attempted.

F. G. JEWETT.

CONTENTS.

CHAPTER I.
EARLY INFLUENCES.   PAGE
The Beginning of Mission Work on Hawaii. — Physical Charms of the Islands. — Birth of Luther Halsey Gulick. — Condition of the People. — Mutual Relation of Missionary and Hawaiian. — Natural Influence of Such Surroundings upon a Child. — Halsey's Ancestry 13

CHAPTER II.
CHILDHOOD.
His Journal. — Indications of Fondness for Study. — Confidence of Others in Him. — His Earliest Friends. — Death of Gerrit Judd 17

CHAPTER III.
AROUND CAPE HORN.
Separation from Home. — His Courage. — Ill Health. — Talcahuano. — Sabbath-keeping. — Working. — His Seriousness. — Arrival at Wood's Holl 25

CHAPTER IV.
IMPRESSIONS OF AMERICA.
Need of Adjustment to New Environment. — Well-intentioned Sabbath-school Superintendent. — Loneliness. — Farm Life in New Jersey and Connecticut. — Introduction to Auburn and to Dr. and Mrs. Halsey 34

CHAPTER V.
SCHOOL LIFE.
Study without Play. — Debating Society. — Appreciation of Time. — His Compositions. — Letter-writing. — Homesickness. — Waiting for Dr. Halsey. — His Reading. — Exhibition and Prizes. — John Quincy Adams in Auburn . . . 46

CHAPTER VI.
SPIRITUAL SUFFERING.

Theological Atmosphere of the Time. — Self-accusation. — Surrounding Conditions. — A Sabbath of Extreme Suffering. — Reading "Baxter's Call." — "A Delusive Hope." — Changed Feelings. — Closing Meditations of the Year 1843 53

CHAPTER VII.
DEDICATION.

Growing Peace. — Pledge of Himself to Foreign Missions. — Preparation for Union with the Church. — Fear of Self-deception. — The Dedication of Himself 65

CHAPTER VIII.
MEDICAL STUDIES.

Indefatigable Study. — Failing Health. — A College Course Impossible. — Medical Study Begun. — Wide Reading. — Desire for Public Speaking. — Depression. — Intimacy with the News of the World. — City Mission Work. — Old Friends and the Meeting of the American Board. — His devotion to Polynesia 72

CHAPTER IX.
FINAL PREPARATIONS.

Theological Study. — Refusal of Proffered Aid. — Projected Mission to Micronesia. — Offer of Himself to the Board. — Doctrinal Perplexities. — His Ordination. — His Marriage. — Louisa Lewis Gulick. — They Sail from Boston . . . 83

CHAPTER X.
FAREWELL.

The Esther May. — The Storm. — Honolulu Again. — Dr. Gulick's Influence upon His Brothers. — Changes among Friends and in the Nation. — Preparation for the Micronesian Mission. — Growing Interest. — Hawaiians Ready to Go as Missionaries. — Purchase of the Caroline. — Public Consecration of the Hawaiian Missionaries. — Kamehameha's Letter. — The Caroline Sails 95

CHAPTER XI.
HAWAII TO KUSAIE.

Discomfort. — Butaritari. — The People. — The King. — Description of a Coral Reef. — Kusaie. — Signs of Civilization. — "Good King George" 110

CHAPTER XII.
REACHING PONAPE.

Excitement of the Crew. — Pictures of the People. — The Welcome. — Mr. Corgat. — Modes of Travel. — The Caroline Leaves 125

CHAPTER XIII.
SMALL BEGINNINGS.

The Ponapeans. — Location of the Missionaries. — Dr. and Mrs. Gulick's Home. — Use of Tobacco in Trade. — Dr. Gulick as Musician. — School work. — Housekeeping. — Building. — Difficulty in Securing Help. — Scarcity of Food . . . 130

CHAPTER XIV.
ISOLATION AND MENTAL ACTIVITY.

Sale of the Caroline. — Irregular Communication with the World. — The Annual Mail. — Disappointments. — His Mental Life. - - The Pressure of Isolation 148

CHAPTER XV.
FURTHER ACQUAINTANCE WITH PONAPE AND HER PEOPLE. — THE EPIDEMIC.

Dr. Gulick's Study of Conditions in Micronesia. — The Outcome of This Work. — Animal Life and Plant Life on Ponape. — The Ruins. — Priests. — The Religion of the People. — The Epidemic 161

CHAPTER XVI.
1857.

General Wakening on Ponape. — The Printing Press. — The First Primer. — Joquin. — Religious Movement. — Dr. Gulick's Desire for more Self-denying Labor 174

CHAPTER XVII.
THE MORNING STAR.

Proposition to Build Her. — Enthusiasm of the Children. — She is Launched. — Ponape Reached. — Mrs. Gulick Returns to Hawaii 182

CHAPTER XVIII.
WAITING.

His Description of Mrs. Gulick. — Life without Her. — Dressmaking. — Letter-writing. — Extracts from Letters to His Wife. — Her Return 188

CHAPTER XIX.
THE CLOSE OF HIS LIFE IN MICRONESIA.

Micronesian Missionaries in 1859. — Proposition to Sell the Morning Star — The Mission Pleads for Her and for Their Work in Micronesia. — Ill Health. — He Returns to Hawaii 196

CHAPTER XX.
CHANGES.

San Francisco Visited. — "The Turning Point" in His Life. — Attends the Meeting of the American Board in Springfield, Mass. — Extended Missionary Campaign among the Churches. — His Pleasure in Speaking. — The Interest of His Audiences. — Invitation to become Secretary of the Board of the Hawaiian Evangelical Association. — His Return to Honolulu 202

CHAPTER XXI.
THE NEW WORK.

Hawaii's Need in 1864. — Lack of Native Pastors. — Reasons for this Condition. — Action of the Hawaiian Evangelical Association in 1863. — Formation of the Board of the Association. — Relation of the American Board to the Hawaiian Board. — Dr. Gulick's Work Outlined. — The Conservatism of Certain Missionaries. — Large Coöperation. — Rapid Results. — Friendship of the Hawaiians. — The Kuokoa. — Visiting among the People 212

CHAPTER XXII.
POLITICS.

Kamehameha IV and Kamehameha V Contrasted. — Proclamation of the King. — Action of the Hawaiian Board. — The Convention. — The King Abrogates the Constitution and Prorogues the Convention. — He gives the People a New Constitution. — Outcome of His Action as Seen in 1893. — News of Abraham Lincoln's Death. — Two Currents in Hawaiian Life. — Two Courses Advocated to Meet the Evil. — Dr. Gulick's Position. — His Arrest by the Government. — The Reprimand 222

CHAPTER XXIII.
TANGLED THREADS.

His Love for both America and Hawaii. — The Variety of His Work. — Results as Shown in 1869. — Kawaiahao Seminary Established. — The Home in Manoa Valley. — The Difficulty of His Position. — His Convictions of Duty. — The Opinion of Others. — He Refuses Reëlection as Secretary of the Hawaiian Board. — Leaves for Boston 236

CHAPTER XXIV.
PAPAL LANDS.

In America Again. — The Scattered Family. — Reversed Plans. — Little Ollie. — To Spain. — Correspondence of the Gulick Family. — Dr. Gulick's Work in Spain. — Spanish Christians and Self-support. — Best Attitude to take toward Spanish Churches. — He goes to Italy. — Hindrances to Work There. — Financial Embarrassment in Boston. — Close of the Italian Mission. — Visit to Turkey. — Return to Boston 247

CHAPTER XXV.
TO THE PACIFIC AGAIN.

His Duties in Boston. — His Desire to Maintain " the Unity of his Life."— A Call from the American Bible Society. — To Japan. — First Impressions. — News of the Death of His Son 261

CHAPTER XXVI.
ADJUSTMENT.
The Pain which Accompanied the Move from One Society to the Other. — Growing Satisfaction in His Work. — Anticipation of His Wife's Arrival. — She Joins Him 266

CHAPTER XXVII.
THE AGED PARENTS.
Reasons for the Move to Japan. — Changes Since They Left America. — The Last Words of Rev. P. J. Gulick. — His Death. — The Death of Mrs. P. J. Gulick 271

CHAPTER XXVIII.
BIBLE WORK.
Work Previously Done by the Bible Society in Japan and China. — Dr. Gulick's Desire to Avoid Giving Pain to Sensitive People. — Departments of Bible Work. — A New Era of Exact Reports Inaugurated. — Rapid Bible Distribution in Japan in 1880. — Division of His Field. — Permanent Location in China. — His Colporters. — His Journeys. — His Thoughts on the Immensity of China. — Bookkeeping. — Progress of the Work 276

CHAPTER XXIX.
OVERWORK.
Preaching in Japan and China. — Character of the Church in Shanghai. — His Audience. — Editorship. — Words of Commendation. — His D.D. — A Son and Daughter Join Foreign Mission Service. — The Call from Hawaii. — Prompt Action in Behalf of Mr. Doane. — His Love for Micronesia. — Quotations Proving Overpressure and Failing Health 289

CHAPTER XXX.
THE END.
Sudden Prostration. — To Japan and America. — Great Suffering. — Continued Weakness. — New York City Again. — Conversation with His Daughter. — His Last Weeks in Springfield. — He Passes Away 304

CHAPTER XXXI.
THE LAST DAYS OF MRS. GULICK.
Desire to Continue in Mission Work. — Visit to the Cemetery. — Return to Japan. — Work There. — Illness. — Death . 310

LUTHER HALSEY GULICK.

CHAPTER I.

EARLY INFLUENCES.

IT was, no doubt, of permanent significance to Halsey Gulick that his earlier years were spent in the midst of the evolution of a Christian from a heathen nation. Missionary work had begun on the Hawaiian Islands in 1820, and the history of that work and of that people is, perhaps, more familiar to the student of missions than that of any other since the days of Paul. Here were islands literally "waiting," and a people who welcomed missionaries with the thrilling words: "Hawaii's idols are no more!"

Added to the attraction of this welcome were the physical charms of Hawaii, for there are mountains here that reach to the snows and valleys so deep that the vines and ferns and moss which drape them hardly know what sunshine is. Here, too, are the whitened outlines of surf upon the sand and the shaded green of rolling breakers, while blue skies and summer clouds are drawn about these islands as a curtain.

Without question, nature and perpetual summer have done their best for Hawaii. But of corresponding comforts of man's making there was painful dearth in Honolulu in June, 1828, when Luther Halsey Gulick was born.[1] Indeed, all that is necessary for real living was still in its infancy here; and though eight years of effort on the part of the earlier missionaries had proved the willingness of the people to improve their condition, Hawaiian barbarism had not, as yet, been exchanged for Western civilization. Natives still lived in unfurnished, straw-thatched houses of primitive fashion, while many of their number were clad in garments even more primitive than their homes. The truth is that these children of the tropics found it a very easy matter to exercise rigid economy in labor and raiment.

Of necessity, the missionaries also lived in simple homes. They had only such comforts as were conveniently brought with them from Boston, around Cape Horn, increased sometimes by the chairs and tables and bookshelves which they themselves took time to make.

Yet neither deficiency in home furnishing nor lack

---

[1] Through childhood he was called Halsey, though in later life he was more often known as Dr. Luther Gulick.

EARLY INFLUENCES. 15

of dainty comforts lessened for Halsey the loving welcome of his parents. Their firstborn son! And this missionary father and mother rejoiced as truly as royalty does when an heir is born. As for the child himself, no palace could have made him merrier and no adornment of " purple and fine-twined linen " could have added any radiance to the love that beamed upon him from his mother's eyes.[1]

Mr. and Mrs. Gulick had reached Honolulu in March, 1828, and thereafter, for forty-six consecutive years, they lived among this people of their adoption — years of prayerful devotion to the good of others.[2]

Now because all the knowledge, the enterprise, the unselfish helpfulness which the Hawaiians had ever seen were centered in the missionary homes multiplying among them, and also because, without any explanation, heathen people know what self-sacrifice

---

[1] Halsey's ancestor, Hendrick Gulick, came to America from the Netherlands in 1653. In 1790 John Gulick was a Christian farmer in New Jersey and his wife was, as they claimed, "the most powerful argument for Christianity" which her seven sons and one daughter had ever known. Peter Johnson, the third son, Halsey's father, was born in 1797. He possessed determination and a lofty ambition, overcame serious obstacles, was graduated from Princeton College in 1825, studied theology there, was married in 1827, and sailed from Boston, in November, as a missionary to the Hawaiian Islands. Fanny Hinckley Thomas, his wife, was of English ancestry, born in 1798 in Lebanon, Conn. While teaching in Utica, N. Y., she was converted by the preaching of Dr. Charles Finney, of Oberlin, and a year later was married to the New Jersey theological student, and sailed with him for Hawaii.

[2] During this time Mrs. Gulick went to California once, but without her husband.

and brotherly love are, very soon and everywhere the missionary was recognized by the natives as their kindest friend. To him they came for medicine, for advice, for instruction, when they were ready for it, for clothing, too, as consciousness of its need dawned slowly upon them. Little by little they were taught to sew, to build better homes, to regard the rights of their neighbors, and to understand the requirement of a righteous God.

In this atmosphere of helpfulness to others — of life devoted to the glory of God and the good of mankind — Halsey Gulick received his first impressions. In his case the forces of a pious ancestry and an environment of self-sacrifice were united, and one need not have been a prophet to foresee the result of this union. Nevertheless unfolding history can alone show whether other forces shall be strong enough to change what seems to be the foreshadowed course of his development.

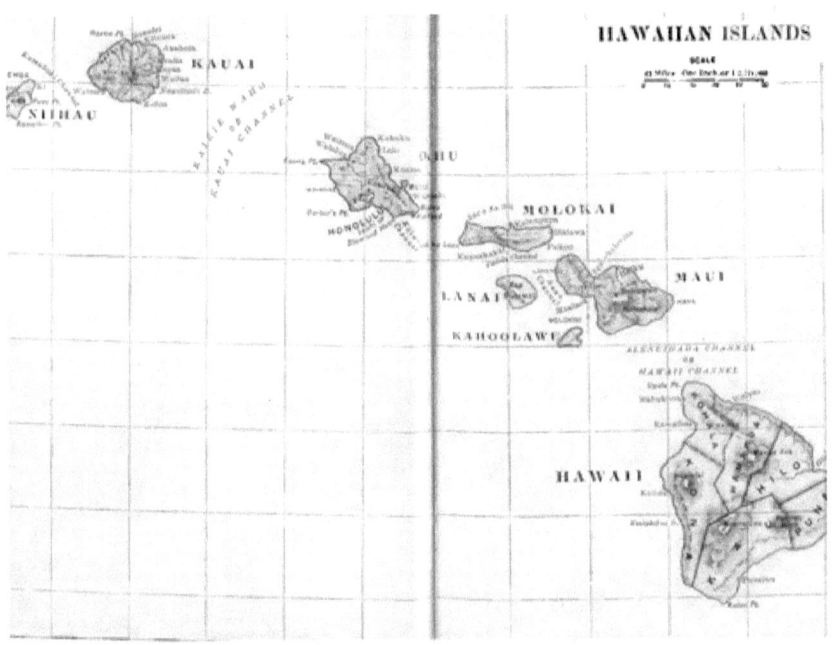

CHAPTER II.

CHILDHOOD.

FOR twenty-five years of his life the material from which we draw our best acquaintance with Halsey Gulick is the journal which he himself kept. This was begun in Koloa, Kauai — where his parents were then stationed — on the twenty-fifth of June, 1836. Halsey was at this time eight years old; and we easily picture the boy as he bent over his square, board-covered first volume and with unaccustomed fingers tried to write in straight lines across unruled pages. To-day the cover is worn, the cramped, childish writing yellow with age. But through all that is written we trace an unfolding life, and see the man already outlined in the boy.

That the scene should be laid on heathen ground adds a certain flavor to the whole. But, curiously enough, the heathen are not mentioned, nor the trees, nor the ocean, nor the splendid climate; probably because for him all this simply represented life in normal conditions. He had known nothing else. There is, however, significant regularity in the daily mention of lessons learned. Indeed the first entry sounds the dominant note of the whole: "Mr. Ladd and son and Mrs. Hooper came to tea. I learnt my lessons before they came." Each succeeding day has its similar story — an item of news, then the cheerful refrain, "I have learnt my lessons." Occasionally, however, there is a minor touch, with the reason for it added: "I have not learnt all my lessons. I helped take care of baby." "I have not learnt my lessons. Mr. Alexander came this morning." Yet in both cases and always through the year 1836 we have laconic brevity.

In December a certain dramatic tendency is added. Tragedy threatens and Halsey's younger brother Orramel is the hero. I give the text in full: —

"December 14. Learnt my lessons. Orramel is sick.

"December 15. Learnt my lessons. Orramel is sick still.

"December 16. Learnt my lessons. Orramel is worse.

"December 17. Learnt my lessons. Orramel is better."

A happy ending, concerning which the youthful scribe doubtless felt more joy than is recorded. But with 1837 there is greater detail. We learn more of studies and daily occupation, as shown in January, when, "It is quite cold this morning," he writes.

"Before breakfast I worked in the garden. At half-past nine I learnt geography, Emerson's Questions, spelling, arithmetic, and writing." Later in the year we read of philosophy added and geometry.

But as yet there is no written sign of emotion or aspiration or struggle with himself. This came as he grew older. Still there is suggestion of it even in 1838 when the year was spent at school in Honolulu. And though the daily journal still tells most of active life, we nevertheless realize by degrees that thoughts are also caught sometimes and given to his journal.

"The day seemed very long," writes the homesick child; and the reason for it follows: "Received some things from home to-day."

Again later: "The scholars did not behave very well in school to-day and I believe Miss Smith felt sad about it."

A footnote to Miss Smith says: "Our teacher." Footnotes, indeed, have become quite helpful to this "clever lad," as his father termed him. So also is another device. To rectify the mistake of a wrongly written word a fresh bit of paper is neatly pasted over it, and on this the word is carefully written. It is very evident that reading and writing already make serious claim on Halsey Gulick and that his instinct is in favor of their best performance. Certainly he is sincere when he says:—

"Miss Smith has gone to Lahaina, and I feel very sorry because there is no school this week."

No doubt there is equal sincerity when he also writes: "It is hard work to keep from whispering and I often yield to the temptation, but I hope I shall be able to very soon overcome."

This is our first introduction to the constantly growing, overmastering purpose of his life, his unflinching determination to be conqueror of himself. Recognizing as we do the moral principle which controlled him, we are not surprised that the mothers in Honolulu used to say: "We always felt perfectly safe when our children were with Halsey Gulick."

Manifestly, friends no less than parents loved the conscientious boy. But something more was required in those stern days. Halsey had not yet passed through the era of spiritual convulsion popularly recognized as "being converted." Without this experience, whatever his life might testify to the contrary, none could feel that his soul was as yet quite safe. Such, indeed, was his own conviction; a conviction pitifully wrought out with pain and tears in later years. The pressure of this requirement is apparent in the letters which now came to him; letters written over fifty years ago and loyally kept till all was over — till the battle had been fought, till life's journey was done. One is from a missionary lady: —

"My dear boy, do you think of these things? Have you felt that you are a sinner against the great, good God? Many little children have given their hearts to God before they were as old as you."

But more precious to him was this other letter — precisely written, neatly folded, faded by the years, worn by its journeyings — this letter from a praying mother in Koloa to her son in Honolulu: —

"We should all be glad to see you. The little boys would talk so much to you and stick so close to you that you would have no time to be lonesome. And your hours of retirement would probably be interrupted. You would have a less favorable opportunity to think of heaven, of hell, of Jesus, and of your own soul than you now have in your little private room. I have hoped that you would give your heart to Jesus in that little room. Oh, how happy we should be if you should come back with a new heart!"

This was part of the influence that molded him, that bore its fruit in later years. But just now in Honolulu life was more full of busy activity than of spiritual contemplation. We are introduced to various young friends — to his dearest schoolmate, Gerrit Judd, and to Sereno Bishop and Hiram Bingham, his lifelong friends.

Besides their mutual occupation, their studies, walks, and games, Halsey had his other interests.

He drew books from the library, borrowed books from his friends, attended lectures when he could, — a very rare treat in those days, — and even exercised himself sometimes in mercantile transactions. Through these we meet again his dear younger brother Orramel.

"I went to Mr. Diell to sell some beans for Orramel; got a shilling for them."

Another venture with other beans brought half a dollar more to himself, Orramel, and John. Then an isolated sentence shows grievous financial loss. Yet it stands without comment or tears: —

"I lost a purse of money with a dollar in it."

Literally a nine days' wonder, for nine days later, again without comment or word of acclamation, this time is the terse sequel: —

"I found my money on the table under some books."

Books already burying out of sight the silver! A significant prophecy.

But Honolulu life came to an end. Halsey returned to Koloa; and the letters which followed him round out for us these early impressions. Two notes from Gerrit are among his treasures of 1839. One of them reads in loving, childish fashion: —

"*Dear Halsey*, — When are you coming to school? for we miss you very much indeed; at least I do."

Following this is a note from their teacher : —

"Gerrit has gone to his long home. His resting place is in the grave till the last trumpet shall wake the slumbering dead. 'Be ye also ready, for ye know not the hour when the Son of Man cometh.' Halsey, are you ready to die? Shall eternal life be your portion or everlasting death? You must not delay your choice. Halsey, give not sleep or slumber to your eyes till you have made your peace with God."

Then the stricken mother writes to Halsey about the last hours of his little friend : —

"He asked to be raised up. The bright sun was just shining into the room. He looked around upon all with a serene, heavenly expression of countenance and then said: 'I feel now that I am going to die and go to heaven. Good-by, dear mother; I shall see you in heaven.' Oh, how our hearts ached all day! At evening it was apparent he was sinking. I bent over him while his breath grew shorter till it was all quite gone and we sang 'Jesus, lover of my soul.' It is very lonely and sad around the house and garden."

Folded closely in this letter is a quaint, old-fashioned locket; and across it, under glass, is a lock of fine hair that gleams in the sunshine and is soft brown in the shadow. On a piece of tinted paper in the familiar penmanship of Halsey's early journals is the added word about it: "A lock of Gerrit's hair, who died November 13, 1839, aged ten years, eight months, and five days."

Notes and locket too have been cherished now for over fifty years. And the gentle presence of the love which treasured them seems very near to them to-day.

CHAPTER III.

AROUND CAPE HORN.

THE scene of the record now shifts. It is October, 1840, and a new heading on a new page introduces us with some formality to new conditions. As if Halsey realized that a crisis in life had come to him, he begins: —

"LUTHER HALSEY GULICK'S JOURNAL, commencing on leaving the Hawaiian Islands for the United States.

"October 2, 1840. Hurry and bustle all day. At four left the abode of my dear parents in Koloa, at the age of twelve years, three months, and twenty-two days, for the land of my forefathers. Shipped aboard the William Penn, Captain Bodfish."[1]

A brief statement, yet only the foreign missionary can understand what it meant to the home in Koloa, to the mother there, and to the eldest son who left it. And even the foreign missionary of to-day must measure with his imagination and not his experience the pain which came with this kind of parting fifty

---

[1] Halsey went in company with Mr. and Mrs. Reuben Tinker and their two sons.

years ago. For in those days separation meant a great chasm seldom bridged. Neither telegraph nor railroad nor ocean steamer had bound the world together. Slow letters exchanged once a year often emphasized the growing estrangement, while parents and children alike were helpless before the inevitable. But duty was as imperative then as now. Innocent children were not safe so close to heathen life. There were two evils to choose between, and wise parents chose the lesser.

For this reason Mrs. Gulick had packed the little trunk while she tried to hide her tears. But her words were brave as she counseled her son, and for the last time prayed with him and in parting whispered; "God bless you, my darling boy, and keep you! Remember that we are praying for you every day." Halsey then sailed away. And after that, for many days, his mother was ill with her grief and could not be comforted.

Through the succeeding eight months we have the story of an ocean voyage on a whaler kept by an earnest little boy who was adapting himself to circumstances and trying to be brave.

An early trial was "the roaches at night" which troubled him. "They bite my toes," he says, "and run over me." This is the way he met the perplexity: "I have a shelf in my berth on which I put my books.

At my feet my clock and bag of clothes are hung up; at my head a borrowed slate — for I forgot to bring one with me — and my Marquesan fan with which I silenced the roaches."

"I feel the need of your help often," he writes to his mother, "but I think I shall learn to think and act for myself after a while." And though through these months of ocean monotony there is no real lamentation of homesickness, still we repeatedly see how much the separation meant to him as well as to his mother, and how constantly his thoughts were with his parents and brothers at home: —

"In the afternoon felt bad in thinking I was leaving home and friends, perhaps never more to see them on earth."

"Passed the Tropic of Cancer yesterday. I can say from my heart there is no place like home."

"Had prayers in the morning for the first time. It brought to my recollection the privileges I enjoyed at home."

"I often think of home, but not with feelings of regret, for I know it is for my good."

Then there is increased pathos: —

"Sundays here do not seem like Sundays at home, for some reason or other. The day seems longer than it used to at home."

"These bright moonlight nights I get up into the

sail that is put up as an awning and think of home and think of getting to the United States."

It is not difficult to imagine the small figure curled up among the sails, and the bright brown eyes that grow dim as they try to span that limitless, moonlit Pacific Ocean, while pictures of home and mother rise before them. But Halsey had determined to be brave; he, therefore, thought also of duty and of the United States. Then, too, there was diversion even on a whaler.

Once his hat flew overboard and there was boyish excitement as a boat hastened after but failed to save it. At times they sighted whales and pursued them. And when they captured one they "took the case on deck and bailed out the oil," while eager eyes "at the masthead saw just how they did it." After all, however, time dragged. Days and weeks moved slowly. Halsey missed the variety of mountain and shore and the freedom of horseback riding, and the journal grows dejected:—

"I feel the need of exercise. I get tired walking."

"Very calm and hot all day. It is very discouraging to be becalmed."

Then for a season he suffers from headache. He stays in bed mornings and neither studies as usual nor writes in his journal. Monday, Tuesday, and Wednesday no longer step with regularity through each recorded week, and we recognize the symptom as serious. But after many days they approached Talcahuano. Here they were to touch before rounding Cape Horn. And now each breeze was full of possibility; each calm a woe; and the days brought every sort of weather: —

"Wind ahead." "Dead calm." "A favorable breeze." "Wind blowing almost a gale." "Very favorable breeze." Then, at last, the small scribe is jubilant: "We have got to Talcahuano harbor. We are anchored, though not in the right place."

Two weeks here involved a new experience in Sabbath-keeping. Now Halsey was not perplexed about the Sabbath question. He had been strictly trained and his pen had thus far followed each Sabbath of the voyage with a quiet notice of it: "Had meeting forenoon and afternoon." "Had meeting twice as usual." "Fine weather; had preaching morning and evening." Then, relentlessly: "No meeting. I wonder at it. Cutting up the whale. It does not seem much like keeping the Sabbath holy." After that, for successive Sabbaths, the simple words: "No meeting," "No meeting," till the condition became chronic and he writes very gravely: "Had no meetings as usual." [1]

[1] Omitted because of Mrs. Tinker's illness. Evidently Halsey did not know the reason.

In Talcahuano there was a difference: —

"We went aboard the frigate Constitution and had services. There was a good deal of noise, though it cannot be helped, for there are five hundred men on board. We had some music. At four we returned, after dining with Commodore Claxton, a kind-hearted old gentleman. Our entertainment was very splendid; far too much so for the Sabbath, I thought."

Those good people did not know how near to them in visible form the recording angel stood, nor how instinctively the divine in the child balanced their professing with their doing. Yet he used his invisible scales every day and made quaint comments sometimes.

"I am rejoiced that I am not a sailor," he writes. "The mate, who professes to be pious, asked one of the men what he was talking about, and the man chose not to tell, so the mate struck him two or three times in the face! This gave great offense to the individual — just as it would to me; therefore he took hold of the mate — just as I should have done, no matter whether he was mate or captain. For this he was turned off duty." Then follows the moral with its childish grammatical twist: "A sailor's life is hard, especially when they have bad masters."

This suggestion of warfare was certainly sinful. Yet it must have been more interesting to a boy than prosaic sewing and washing. He nevertheless did the prosaic thing, and turning it into recorded history one day he writes:—

"Sewed a little." Then again: "In the evening washed some clothes." And later: "I feel pretty tired; washed six shirts, three towels, one pair of trowsers, aired my bed, put my woollen clothes to the bottom of my chest." Diligent boy of twelve!

After leaving Talcahuano he was still more diligent, for now he added the duties of cabin boy to his other occupations. This he was glad to do, as it was through the personal kindness of Captain Bodfish that he was able to go to America on this whaler.

"I like my business of steward very well," he writes one day. "I rise at five in the morning and set the table, set the table at eleven for dinner and four for supper." But later the pleasure of it passes, for "it is pretty cold now," he says. "It is not so comfortable to get up in the morning as it used to be." Then there is added trouble: "I have to take great care when I go with the dishes, it is so rough." "A heavy gale blowing. The wind made a great noise whistling through the rigging. Headlights in."

Verily no imagination is needed to recognize the serious tone of these early journals. It is not brooding melancholy, not weakness, but as if even this lad had looked with unclouded eye into life and recognized its great significance. Sometimes, indeed, there are amusing situations. Yet even then only a smile is caught between the lines, never any laughing. In fact the nearest approach to a merry note is when he says: —

"I have been securing my things so that they may not 'fetch away' as the sailors say. I am getting quite inclined to speak as the sailors do."

But several months later, in a footnote to this entry, he thus chides himself for the unusual levity: "This is the day on which Lucy Thurston left this world, as is hoped, for a better one. How different would have been my thoughts and my occupation had I known that while I was so thoughtlessly spending my time the spirit of the lovely missionary daughter was winging its flight to another world!"

At last, however, it is May, 1841. The end of the voyage is near; and in its ending, as in its beginning, we feel the throbbing patriotism of this boy for the land he had never seen. With a certain solemnity as if he wrote, "Thus endeth the first lesson," he makes his closing entries: —

"We are drawing near the land of my forefathers, but not my home."

"Friday, May 28. In the morning at four o'clock got a pilot and went into the Sound. At about a quarter before nine o'clock got to anchor in Wood's Holl. At eleven went to Captain Fisher's with Samuel Tinker. So we have reached the end of our voyage after a passage of two hundred and thirty-eight days, or eight months lacking three days."

CHAPTER IV.

IMPRESSIONS OF AMERICA.

WHEN Halsey landed at Wood's Holl, near New Bedford, he was filled with curiosity concerning the United States, and he also had exalted anticipation of things that were better than those he had left. For thus far the highest civilization he had seen was that of Hawaii, in 1840, and the only Christianity he had ever known was that which had given itself to foreign missionary work. Christian men with lives spent in money-making he had never met. This was part of the new thing which America held for him. Guided by less noble aims than the uplift of a nation, Christian life in the central Pacific would have seemed puerile — unworthy.

Stamped by the early environment, Halsey had come to the new. To it he must adjust himself. Indeed, with each new experience there was inevitable adjustment, and often the process was painful. Yet the actual must replace the ideal. Despite its odd mixture of well-meant kindness and unintentional cruelty, humanity in America must be accepted as he found it.

A lesson in this direction came soon after landing.

It is not recorded in his journal. Perhaps the pain was too deep to be repeated at the time in writing. And yet we know that young Gulick never forgot the sense of astonishment and humiliation which it brought to him one Sabbath morning.

He was at Sabbath-school; and the worthy superintendent, with more kindness than delicacy, told the children about the little missionary boy who had come to them from a heathen land. To prove the need that his benevolent plan should be carried out, he showed to the school the hat which Halsey Gulick wore, and then proposed that they give him money enough to buy another. So the small hat from Hawaii, the travel-worn hat that was not very modern, was passed about to gather up the pennies.

No doubt it was the old, unpardonable blunder of ignorant sinning — intentions being truly kind — yet the grief which followed was none the less real to the child who endured it. The new world had suddenly grown cold, and lonely too. And to emphasize the loneliness, it was almost a month before he reached his relatives and could once more feel that he really belonged to anybody. This interval of time represented a few days with Mr. and Mrs. Tinker at Wood's Holl; separation from these last of the home friends; sail by slow schooner to New York; a brief visit there with his mother's old friend, Mr. Ripley; then, with a sigh and a tear of disappointment perhaps, the significant words : " So ends the third week in the land of my ancestors."

By slower schooner yet he went to Forked River, New Jersey, and records another Sabbath and a birthday on the water : —

" Sabbath we passed Hell Gate. I helped pull at the oars, thinking it would be no sin, for we might get against the rocks."

" To-day is my birthday. How different I should spend it with my dear parents ! "

Precious boy ! And your mother that day, on distant Kauai, was praying as only a mother can pray, that God would comfort her son. It would be yet five months before she could hear that he had safely reached her home; and Halsey in turn would not hear from his mother until a year after he had left her. Those were brave, hard days for mother and son alike; for her in imagination of what might be; and for him in realization of what was.

Solitary traveling to new places in a strange land was a dreary experience. No friends accompanied him ; none met him at any point. All were kind when he reached them, but the boy in the " land of his forefathers " was homeless and utterly alone. He did not complain in his journal, no doubt accepting it all as part of the new life. But in later years Dr. Gulick spoke sometimes of that first great loneliness and the desolateness of it. The worst ended, however, when, with a renewed sense of the dramatic, he wrote: —

"Got into harbor at six this morning. At seven went ashore. After walking about two miles I found the house I had been looking for for about nine months. Found my uncle and aunt well."

Farm life in New Jersey and Connecticut introduced Halsey at once to a world of new creatures and experiences. Everything was full of interest and much had its "first time" for him.

"Saw a toad for the first time," he says. "Strange-looking creatures but just as they are represented in books."

"This morning killed a snake, the second and largest one I ever saw."

"To-day I was much pleased with the novelty of riding on the hay."

But most delightful of all: "Last night Aunt Eliza had a little son. It is the first cousin I ever saw. Did nothing all day but run around and talk of my cousin."

Halsey himself, with his thoughtful words and earnest ways, not to mention his box of curiosities, must have been interesting to his relatives. And then his clothes! In addition to the fashion of them there was the demoralized condition that followed shipboard use, and his own pitiful attempt at washing. This inspired more dismay perhaps than interest in the heart of his aunt, for "when we opened my chest and box," he says, "aunt thought my clothes looked very dirty. She can have no idea of an eight months' voyage aboard a whaler."

Soon, however, "Betsey Harry" and "Betsey Clark" are recorded as having "come to make my clothes." The wardrobe is in shape again. Halsey has visited the old home in Connecticut, "truly a place which is not to be despised," as he testifies; and now school life in America is before him.

"October 27, 1841. Started for Auburn this morning at three o'clock. I rode all day and reached here (Albany) at eleven o'clock in the evening. I got pretty tired."

"Thursday, 28. Got to Auburn at ten o'clock in the evening, having left my trunk at Syracuse by accident. But I think I shall get it again. P.M. Went to the depot when the cars came in and found my trunk. It was all safe. Took a walk around town. This village is a very pleasant place."

Thus had Halsey traveled alone once more to meet new faces in a new place. For the present, however, this ended his journeyings. He had come to Auburn to find his permanent home with Dr. Luther Halsey, his father's friend of Princeton days. It was for him that Luther Halsey Gulick was named, and with him that much of his time in the United States was spent. He was a wise counselor and a kind friend always. Mrs. Halsey was no less kind, and Halsey loved them both. And yet, through these early years, no friend became so intimate with him as to intercept the confidences which found increasing fullness of expression in his journal. This loss of intimate human friendship no doubt explains much of the mental suffering which came to him later in lines of religious thought.

CHAPTER V.

SCHOOL LIFE.

REMEMBERING that even in Honolulu school had its charm for him, we imagine the eager expectancy with which Halsey reached his first school home in America, and entered in due form the Auburn Academy. Still we must imagine this, for it does not appear in the manuscript. What we really apprehend is the necessity he felt for immediate adaptation to an astonishing schoolroom emergency : —

"There is so much noise I cannot study, but I hope to get used to it soon."

Later we note a quiet satisfaction in his small room in the attic, "because it is so entirely removed from any noise"; his growing passion for books; his grief when holidays, vacations, or illness interfere with his studies; and his written protest against "not needed liberties" when, because it is hot, school is "dismissed earlier than usual," and "lessons shortened."

In fact, he carried his devotion to such a point that for months after he went to Auburn we search in vain for some sign of outdoor exercise, or sports with other children. At last the silence is explained : —

"To-day for the first time I played a game of football; feel pretty tired. It is the first time I have played since I have been here."

Thirteen years old, and this the first time he had played in six months! Still he was not wholly without diversion. He piled wood for exercise sometimes. And there was promise of much pleasure when he joined a debating society. But early convictions were strong. Profanity shocked him. He soon left, saying, —

"My reason for leaving it was the use of profane and vulgar language. Some think me too scrupulous about it. But my parents have often told me that the less I have to do with those who use profane language, the better. When I joined them I thought them to be young men in morals as well as in size; but I find that I was greatly mistaken, for I have never heard worse language used wherever I have been, not excepting shipboard."

This unhesitating allegiance to what seemed duty is constantly seen. Yet there is also frequent self-accusation. We are often led to anticipate the confession of serious wrongdoing, until with a start of surprise we suddenly realize that the grievous reproach of this mere child is not for actual sin committed, but over time which he thinks he has wasted; as on the first of January, 1842: —

"Another year has passed," he says, "never to return. Oh, I have done a great many things for which I am ashamed! I have disobeyed God all of the past year, and I cannot dare to hope that he will keep me another year if I keep on in the same way. Let me reform and try to live better this year — I mean improve my time. My motto for this year shall be 'Redeem the time.'"

Indeed, through these years, whatever else is wanting in the journal, there is no lack of proof that thoughts of time, of life, its importance and its brevity were constantly with him: —

"To-day is my dear father's birthday. He is forty-five years old. How fleeting is time! It is even like a vapor that appeareth for a little while and vanisheth away. The time will soon arrive, if I live, when I shall be as old as my father. Yet how distant it seems!"

And later: "This is the close of the year, and I have been spending it in making a 'fox and geese' board. My conscience reproves me for it. There are ways, almost without number, that I might have spent it more profitably. But it is too late. The day has gone, weeks have gone, months too, and years. They have gone, never to return. How solemn the thought!"

In the meantime, however, proofs that Halsey did

improve his moments are before us in writing. What tales they tell!

Here is his first literary effort. It greets the world neither as "Essay" nor "Paper," but states its modest aspirations as "Intended for a Composition." With it are many other compositions, all carefully written, all numbered in regular order, all tied neatly in one package. Some carry the ordinary titles under which the ordinary youth most often writes. Others are index fingers of the writer himself. One enumerates the steps of "The Staircase of Knowledge," steps which we easily see that he himself is climbing. Another assails without apology "Fashion, the Child of the Devil." And with drawn sword this child from heathen lands denounces the goddess whom we follow. He calls her "a thief," "a swindler," "an outcast of hell"; the "meanest of devils and the proudest of devils," "the gravest of devils and the merriest of devils," "the worst of devils and the most fascinating of devils."

Verily, he is in earnest with his convictions. And the voice of his young aspiration rings out no less earnestly in his unformed, youthful sermon on "What we are, What we might be, and What we will be": —

"Fellow students, we may be great and good men, and we may be ignorant and vile men. We may be a blessing to society and we may be a disgrace to it. We may live in obscurity unknown and uncared for; we may be looked up to when living and spoken of when dead with veneration. . . . Determine in your own mind what you will be, and then pursue it. Be not deterred by trifles or by obstacles, however great. . . . Determination is a potent charm. It has an irresistible power. When put in motion it sweeps all before it. It is like a flood. It carries before it all the dams of indolence and the bridges of folly. It overwhelms all the castles of self-esteem and widens the channels of fearful cautiousness."

In addition to this writing of compositions a time-worn memorandum book brings to us a record of all letters written and received between 1840 and 1848. Dates are faithfully noted. The years stand by themselves. Words of explanation are introduced. All entries are in ink and neatly written. And through it, from first page to last, are the names of father and mother, of Orramel, John, Charles, William, Theodore, and Thomas — so large a family that in referring to a letter received he says: —

"My brothers were all well, and the oldest six of them (too long a list to enumerate!) were at Punahou boarding school."

Family birthdays were also remembered, and we sometimes feel the homesickness which swept as a deep undercurrent to his life; peculiarly so on a brother's birthday, when he says: —

"Such days as this in particular my mind leaves the location of the body and seems to travel away eighteen thousand miles to my parents and my brothers, and I vainly wish I knew how they were spending it. But as I cannot know,

> 'Fond memory brings the light
> Of other days around me,'

and I fancy that they are celebrating it in the same manner as we did in 'other days.' Yet frequently the thought will intrude itself into my mind: 'Perhaps they are mourning the loss of one of their number. Or, perhaps, — unwelcome thought, — there is no one left of them all, either to mourn or rejoice.'"

Then as a sad refrain to his thinking, the song in full is written out: —

> Oft in the stilly night,
>   Ere slumber's chain has bound me,
> Fond memory brings the light
>   Of other days around me:
> The smiles, the tears
>   Of boyhood's years,
> The words of love then spoken;
>   The eyes that shone,
>   Now dimmed and gone.
> The cheerful hearts now broken!

> Thus in the stilly night
>   Ere slumber's chain has bound me,
> Sad memory brings the light
>   Of other days around me.
>
> When I remember all
>   The friends so linked together,
> I've seen around me fall
>   Like leaves in wintry weather,
> I feel like one
>   Who treads alone
> Some banquet hall deserted,
>   Whose lights are fled,
> Whose garlands dead,
>   And all but he departed!
>
> Thus in the stilly night
>   Ere slumber's chain has bound me,
> Sad memory brings the light
>   Of other days around me.

Yet homesickness in a child's heart is not always dominant, nor always tearful. It is often hidden by busy occupation or delightful sport. Thus it was with Halsey. Vacations in New Jersey were full of swimming and driving, and farming and rest. But when they came to an end he was "not the least sorry for it," as he says, "because all play suits me no better than it did Jack."

Without any question he preferred study to play. And for this reason an experience which came to him one fall was peculiarly trying.

SCHOOL LIFE. 47

He had returned to Auburn as directed by his guardian, and had learned that Dr. and Mrs. Halsey were expected the next day. With much excitement and pleasure he therefore went to the station the next day to meet them. We feel the contagion of suppressed excitement as the alert, slender boy with bright hair and brown eager eyes watches the train as it comes, and then stands breathless to welcome his friends.

His eyes were not so bright and his step was slower as he went home that evening, for his guardians had not come. He had the same experience the next day and the next. In fact it was repeated without variation every day for six weeks. School had begun, but he must not enter till Dr. and Mrs. Halsey should arrive. Worst of all, no letter came to explain, and no directions as to what this fatherless, motherless boy should do. He was boarding, and a few extracts from his journal show how time dragged: —

"Paid my usual visit to the depot. As usual did not find Dr. Halsey."

"Time passes very slowly, or at least seems to. I go to the depot once or twice every day, partly to spend the time, but chiefly in hopes Dr. Halsey will come."

"This week like the rest has been spent in reading, writing, and going to the depot."

"This long vacation ought, I think, to suffice for

some time to come, as it is a great hindrance to a student to relinquish his studies long at a time."

At last, however, a letter came from Dr. Halsey. They had been unavoidably detained by the illness of Mrs. Halsey. "He hopes," writes the lad, "I will not take up too many studies, and cautions me against confining myself too closely."

Halsey entered the Academy at once, and, compensating himself for the long vacation, he studied persistently through seventeen of the succeeding nineteen months in Auburn.

Glancing backward for a moment, we appreciate the value of books to him while he waited. He seems to have read constantly; not with an unreasoning devotion to whatever he found that was written, but with such guidance of his instinct that the profitable and not the foolish was chosen. Granted that at fourteen a boy's instincts may not always be trusted, still the sort of admiration given is some measure of the kind of books that please him. And at this time Halsey showed his line of choice in the inspiration that came to him through D'Aubigne's History of the Reformation.

"I am much pleased with the two principal characters which figured in the Germanic Reformation, Luther and Melanchthon, though I hardly know which to admire most, Luther for his boldness, or Melanchthon for his mildness. I think, however, I should prefer being a Luther (I am one by name). There is something noble, something that evinces more than ordinary courage, in the act of standing up before the crowned heads of the earth, whose decisions will, perhaps, consign one to the fate of a martyr, and fearlessly announcing and defending one's doctrines, something which makes me sometimes wish that I had lived in that age, and could have taken part in those transactions. But those days are past, and I must prepare for usefulness in some other sphere, though it may be that I shall yet have a similar opportunity to ascertain what spirit I am of."

A hope that erelong proved to be a prophecy. He showed indeed, even then, the spirit that was in him by the disapproval which flashed itself across events or doings that seemed to him unworthy, insincere — as concerning a Fourth of July celebration : —

"How greatly have we honored our fathers who procured us that in which we glory! With what complacency must Washington now be looking on us who have forgotten the 'God of battles'! Why not render tribute to whom tribute is due? Bacchus cannot be the author of our independence."

Annual examinations followed. Life grew more intense, and Halsey's scorn of all sham, of all performing for appearance is increasingly manifest : —

"There is great excitement nowadays about the 'Old Hospital' as, in common parlance, we term the academy. Examination is near at hand, and though the fate of each individual is, ere this, decided, there is something rousing to some minds in that it is soon to be known and that in public. Certain portions of the book with which we are already quite familiar are selected as those in which we are to be examined! And thus we are to aid in increasing the reputation of the academy! A ridiculous imposition on the public and the parents of those attending there.

"There was no school to-day, so as to give the little urchins an opportunity to breathe the fresh air and clean themselves preparatory to the wonderful examination. A greater account could not be made of the greatest exhibition imaginable than is of this vexatious examination. I, however, feel very little concern or anxiety about any appearance or show. I shall perform my part as well as I can, and trouble myself no farther."

Then came the exhibition — the marching two by two, decorated with badges, preceded by martial music and followed by teachers, trustees, and citizens; the exercises in the First Church, and then the climax of it all — the prizes.

I wonder if it grieved those merry boys and girls that the stranger among them should receive more than they all. Was it hard for them to understand that this quiet boy from Hawaii who studied when they played, who thought when they were thoughtless — that this boy, so much less American than they by birth, was yet more truly American than most of them in noble love for America, in devotion to duty, in improvement of opportunity? Perhaps neither they nor he appreciated yet the difference. Certainly there is no self-conscious approval in the simple record: —

"There were in all sixteen speakers, and the best speaker received a premium selected for that purpose. After all had finished came the distribution of premiums. I received three: 'The Orator's Own Book' for algebra, 'Holiday Tales' in writing, and 'Croley's Selections from British Poets' for the best speech of the whole. My spirits and strength have been screwed up to this point, and now they give way. I am as completely deprived of any youthful vivacity as I ever was. These examinations do not agree with me. So farewell, school; welcome, welcome vacation!"

The great event of this vacation was a visit to Auburn by John Quincy Adams; and Halsey's spirited account of the affair throws a new touch of color into the picture he is painting of himself: —

"As soon as Mr. Adams entered the church there was a general rush for good seats. And as every one pushed and ran, I pushed and ran also, so that, by jumping one seat I got to the nearest possible seat to the stage. The stage was the one on which we made our speeches." Then in parenthesis there is the shrewd deduction, "The statesman and orator is but little removed from the schoolboy."

". . . After he had finished speaking, when about halfway down the aisle, a little child two or three years old attracted his notice, which he immediately lifted up and kissed, to the infinite amusement of those assembled. After that I saw several mothers trying to get their children into his notice, but all 'the little children' were not 'suffered to come unto' him. Seeing so many pressing forward to shake hands, many smaller than myself, and as I knew the ceremony to be a simple one, the spirit of enthusiasm was infused into my veins, and I pressed forward also to receive a share of the blessing. I can now say to the day of my death: 'I have seen John Quincy Adams and shaken hands with him'!"

Vacation came to an end. The boy was rested and eager for school. And reversing the refrain of a month before, he now writes: "Farewell vacation. Welcome, welcome school."

CHAPTER VI.

SPIRITUAL SUFFERING.

RUNNING parallel with his school life and, indeed, closely interwoven with the history of it, is the very sad story of the spiritual suffering through which Halsey was at the same time passing. The pathos of the minute journal record of it is the fact, which seems evident from the beginning, that he was a Christian through the whole of it, and that the questioning, the self-distrust, the torment of mind and soul which he endured were but the natural outcome of a morbid theology fermenting in the mind of a highly organized, self-depreciative child. It was, indeed, on a sternly anthropomorphic view of God that he was spiritually nurtured; a theology which emphasized the wrath of God and the horrors of hell, and finally, as a test question, asked him whether, "If he knew he were doomed to hell, he would still determine to serve God?"

In turning these yellow pages we are increasingly impressed by the fact that Halsey's soul was utterly alone when he wrote them. His parents were so far away that no letter could receive its answer in less than a year. His relatives in this country were necessarily strangers to him. Of his kindest friends Dr. Halsey was an overworked professor and Mrs. Halsey an invalid. His journal was, therefore, his only confidant, and through it we are able to follow the soul of a child as it gropes its way to God alone. The struggle began in 1842.

"The Holy Spirit has been striving with me lately," he writes, "but I have resisted it. I would not have God to reign over me; I sometimes think I really wish to be forgiven and have a new heart, yet I know my unwillingness is all that hinders me. I hardly know what to do. I am told to pray, but I cannot; I can speak, it is true, but that is all. I do not feel penitent. I am afraid to die, afraid of God, and of the torments of hell, where I know I shall go, if I die as I am now."

This was the beginning of the suffering which reached its climax almost a year later. Concerning the closing three months of the year he says:—

"My time was so at my own disposal during the whole of this period that I could make no excuse with respect to opportunities for reflection. I was six hours at school and almost the whole of the remainder of the day I had to myself. Mrs. Halsey was not at home and Dr. Halsey being absent at the seminary a great part of the time, I frequently sat for hours

SPIRITUAL SUFFERING.   55

in their room, engaged in reading and reflection. My feelings were disclosed to no one, nor have they been to this day, save in a letter to my parents."

We are thus made acquainted with surrounding conditions, and they show very little physical exercise, practically no companions, because he did not care for the usual sports of children, no older counselor, an intense Calvinistic theology, of which he had grasped more than does the ordinary child of fifteen, a keen imagination, sensitive conscience, and consecutive hours and days and weeks for self-examination, self-accusation, and pain. The results which followed were to be expected. Indeed, given the conditions, one might have predicted the result.

" From the twenty-second of October to the tenth of December," he continues, " my feelings were such as never before or since. For the first few days I felt scarce any interest at all in things not immediately connected with religion. My studies afforded me no pleasure or relief. I envied the birds and inanimate objects their state; and I do not know but truth will warrant me in saying I in reality thought myself no longer ' a prisoner of hope!'

"It surprised me that my fellow students who were not professed Christians could be so thoughtless and trifling when hell was before them."

At this time he passed through a crisis of emotion which he describes as "agony."

"October 22, 1843. I arose this morning as usual a little before six and aided in the necessary labors of the commencing day. After breakfast I occupied myself by reading in my Bible, and as I read I began seriously to think whose service I should enter, the service of God or of Satan. Had any one asked me which I should prefer dying in the service of, or which I really intended to be the servant of, I should unhesitatingly have replied: 'That of God'; and it was indeed my intention to choose him; but before doing so formally I thought it proper to count the costs, that I might clearly understand what I took upon myself.

"Before commencing, however, I knelt and prayed — was it prayer? — that I might have a true idea of the Christian duties and that the Holy Spirit might aid me in my decision. I then attempted to 'call in my wandering thoughts' and collect my mind, that I might not go heedlessly and ignorantly to work.

"My mind ran over several of the duties which would be required of me and which the world, as well as God, would expect me to perform; but in some way now forgotten my attention was called off. I began to think about other things, and my attention was not arrested till the bells began to ring for morning service, when I went to my room to get my cloak preparatory to going. But suddenly as I was putting on my cloak 'I AM LOST' crowded itself among my truant thoughts. 'I am lost. I did not choose God and his service. My day of grace is past.' Such thoughts as these rushed upon me like a torrent, and so powerfully did the thought force itself upon my mind, an effort did not shake it off.

"I paused a moment in the act of placing the cloak on my shoulders. I knew not what to think of it. At first I attempted not to heed it, as I perceived it began to agitate me greatly. But I could not divert my mind. I experienced such sensations in those few moments as I hope never to have again. They were of horror and fear. I was in the greatest agitation. I cannot with words, and particularly on paper, describe my feelings. Perspiration began to start from my brow. And in my agony I knelt down by my bed to implore, if it were possible, mercy from Him whom I had offended. But I found it impossible. I could not summon my wandering thoughts together. And then the idea of addressing him was not connected with any hope. For how could I hope for mercy from one I had so deeply offended?

"This all passed through my mind in the space of five minutes, when I joined the family going to the house of God. When walking, my mind was a little drawn off, but looking on passing objects I felt as if I should never behold them with pleasure and gayety as before. In church my feelings rose to their former intensity and, if possible, higher. I could not sit still and heard but detached portions of the sermon.

"My feelings did not rise again during the day, but they were of a melancholy character and so continued, effecting nothing because 'there was no hope and no use in attempting.'"

After this Halsey suffered every day. There was, it is true, fluctuation in his feelings, degrees of intensity to the pain. Yet the pain itself was constant. He believed that if he were not living in such hardened rebellion against God, no day would pass without definite thought on what he terms "the lost condition" of his soul. That days did thus pass was proof to himself that he had outlived all possibility of repentance, that he had sinned away his "day of grace"; and his suffering was measured by the enormity of this calamity.

The prevailing tone of the journal during these months is best shown when he began to read Baxter's Call.

"In commencing this book," he writes, "I have a variety of feelings. I almost fear to read it, lest, through the extreme and wonderful hardness of my heart, I should still continue in my sins, and thus it should prove a 'savour of death unto death.'

"It is with the greatest surprise that I look at myself. I know that I must die, that I am a sinner, that I cannot escape deserved punishment but by closing in with the offers of mercy made by the only begotten Son of the Father, and I believe I understand the way of salvation; yet there is something, I know not what, unless it is my wicked heart, which prevents me, and which I have reason to fear will be my ruin.

"What infatuation! 'T is sufficient to terrify the boldest sinner. And yet I walk on, on the very margin of the lake which burneth with fire and brimstone, as careless and unconcerned as though with the fool I said 'There is no God and no soul.' Well may the angels look and be astonished! Not all my guilt subdues me, nor my great danger, nor yet the compassion of a Redeemer in dying, nor the unparalleled long-suffering of a merciful God. 'Oh! wretched man that I am!' my sins increasing, my heart hardening, my time shortening, death approaching, hell gaping, and my doom preparing! Nothing but the grace of God can save me. 'Create in me a new heart,' and make me what thou wouldst have me to be."

Then soon after:—

"At times I imagine I am given up of God, and I feel a sort of melancholy despair, while at other times

I am in great agony. Yet, after all these fears and resolves and, I cannot but hope, strivings of the Spirit, I continue in my sins, in my extraordinary rebellion against my Maker, so that I have good ground to fear that I have grieved or shall grieve away the Spirit and be forever lost. Oh, may this never be the case with me! May I see my many sins in something of that light in which God sees them! I do not realize the state I am in, or I could take no peace day or night."

Through these months of keen introspection not a breath of hope had reached him; and the depth of his woe, as we have seen, was the agonized desire of his soul for repentance and forgiveness and the belief that, in spite of himself, the hardness of his heart alone prevented peace and pardon. To himself his case seemed hopeless, and he blamed himself alone.

At last, however, hope came to him for a moment, "a delusive hope" he sadly called it; and though in simple words that have no hope in them he tells us how it came and how it went again, still we see at once a promise and a sign that day is approaching : —

"On Sabbath, the tenth of this month," he writes, "after the tea dishes were removed and the family worship over, Mr. Seymour, a theological student, requested me to remain a few moments. He asked me if I would kneel down with him and promise God that I would serve him and from that time forward live wholly for him. I hesitated. I knew not what to do. I was unprepared for it. It was reasonable. It was what I ought to do. Yet I dared not do it. It would be more correct should I say I would not. My blood rushed into my face. I was greatly excited and it was with difficulty I could bring my mind to think on it for a moment.

"My mind reverted to my feelings on the twenty-second of October. The thought occurred to me: 'There still is hope. If you repent now, you may be saved, and this may be the last time the Spirit will ever strive with you; the last opportunity you will ever have.' I tried to collect my thoughts to make an effort, but could not. The frequency of my making such resolves came up. I thought these would be like the rest, mere words or thoughts, not the firm resolves of the heart. As I said then: 'I dare not say No, yet cannot say Yes;' I could not come to any decision.

"We then knelt down. Mr. Seymour offered prayer and I followed him; after which he advised me to retire to my room and give myself away unreservedly.

"I was occupied during the evening with my own thoughts. I ran over the ground several times, counting the costs, and brought myself to the point whether I would or would not do it, which I answered in the affirmative. After this point was settled in my mind

I went alone and, as I thought, yielded my heart to God, and, as I hope, resolved to seek and strive to enter into the kingdom of heaven.

"My feelings now assumed a very different aspect. They were entirely changed. Instead of feeling that I was lost, I was full of joy and hope. I felt as a new creature, and was tempted to hope that I was a Christian. Since then I have passed day after day with an indefinite hope. I have scarcely dared bring myself to the test, lest I should find my heart not right before God, till yesterday, when I think I found sufficient to disperse all such hope. Every day reveals more and more the deceitfulness of my own heart. And yet I have been flattering myself that I was a child of God and an heir of heaven!"

Five days later we read the closing words of the closing year. As usual I quote but a small part of what is written: —

"Sunday, December 31, 1843. It is ten o'clock. But two hours remain of 1843. Soon another year will have commenced. But who knows whether I shall live to see it? Oh, who? None but God. Let me then improve the remaining part of the year in meditation.

"I have lately indulged in the hope that I have received pardon for my sins. I have, however, after much thought not discovered sufficient evidence to induce me to rely on it. No, I fear I am still unreconciled to God, that he is still angry with me. It is just. It is proper. But how can I remain a moment in peace? Is God angry with me and I not concerned? God displeased with me and I insensible? This is a mystery. There are, however, moments when I am really tempted to believe I am a child of God. I can think of nothing then as a test but which corresponds, as I think then, with my feelings. I then look forward to the judgment day and think that, through the blood of Christ, I need fear nothing. I think of death, and picture to myself a peaceful departure from this world. But oh, the thought will intrude itself, for it is indeed unwelcome: 'What if this is all a delusion! You may yet be in your sins. Satan may only be deceiving you with these vain hopes, the better to secure you as his victim.' Yes, and this may be true. It is in truth the most probable supposition. Oh, what am I to do if this be the case? I am lost! *I am lost!* I AM LOST!

"The clock strikes eleven. Only one hour left! And if the end of this year is to be the close of my earthly career, how soon will it close? This may be the case. The decree may have gone forth with respect to me: 'Cut it down. Why cumbereth it the ground? Behold, these fifteen years I come seeking fruit on this fig tree and find none.'

"And what will be my condition in the future world? I pause to address myself to my Maker, my Saviour, my Redeemer. May he in his infinite mercy deliver me from my uncertainty, and may I be brought to action before it shall be forever too late! . . .

"But the year has gone. Its last moments have fled. It has gone. Its accounts are sealed for eternity. And what a record will they present at the last day! One that I shall be pleased with? Ah! no. It will present one continual sin. All its pages are blackened with sin — sin against the Almighty. It has gone . . . 'with the days beyond the flood.'

"May my New Year's present to the Lord be ' my body a living sacrifice, holy, acceptable unto God, which is my reasonable service.'

"LUTHER HALSEY GULICK.
"January 1, 1844. Midnight."

CHAPTER VII.

DEDICATION.

AS the sobs of a child grow gradually fainter and then are changed to smiles, so it happened with Halsey's spiritual suffering. It did not cease at once. Peace came to him slowly. There were seasons of discouragement when he deplored his weakness, his coldness, his unfaithfulness. And finally, having overcome much, he shuddered in the imagined presence of a new tormenting specter — spiritual pride.

After all, however, the real contest was between the powers of spirit and intellect. Each claimed his highest devotion. As rivals they already stood within the citadel, and now one and now the other was its master. And yet the higher power proved itself the stronger. For under and over and about all else was the spiritual yearning of his life — the note which sounds as an insistent undertone to all he writes. This is very distinctly heard when he announces as his "Christian axiom" the duty of each human being to choose his life work "where talent and circumstances will enable him most to glorify God."

Because of this conviction, with all life and its possibilities before him, he dedicates himself to foreign missions. His reasons are the willing nations, the greater need, the hopeful work; while shining as a calcium light over all is the example of his parents.

"Were reasons valid in their case," he exclaims, "which are not in mine? Shall it be said that the son of a missionary was so dandled on the lap of ease and indulgence that he thinks it a hard matter to make sacrifice for his God; that the son of a missionary is not so good a missionary as the son of a New Jersey farmer or the daughter of a Puritan? Was the command 'Go ye into all the world' addressed more particularly to my parents than to me? I answer to each and all a conscience-approving 'No.'"

Such was the inspiration from his parents! But there was loyalty also to heathen neighbors.

"I was born among the heathen," he says. "They are, as it were, my countrymen. And now shall I forsake them? No: to a certain degree I will claim the whole heathen world as my countrymen."

Thus, quite unconsciously, did Halsey prophesy of his future. And thus soberly did he take his place with the workers of the world.

"I must now be a man," he continues with unassumed gravity. "I must be sober, stable, persevering, living for eternity — which is the part of true manliness. I must acquire complete control over my thoughts. This I have not. I must be rigid in my self-examination and thorough in my self-knowledge. I would live, as Brainard expresses it, 'on the brink of eternity.' My communion with God must be close."

These were lofty aspirations sincerely held. Yet side by side with them there was constant fear of self-deception. And to help him answer the question of his own honesty he read "The Deceived Professor Undeceived." After that he writes: —

"It seemed to me as if my submission was for the sake of pardon; as if my love — if indeed I exercised any — was because I thought I was to be saved."

For further help he now went to a friendly theological student; and here he met with the astonishing query as to whether "if he knew he were doomed to hell, he would be determined still to love and serve God." This was no astonishment to himself, however, for it harmonized with what he already believed and it therefore helped him. Later he talked with Dr. Halsey, met the session of the church, passed the church examination, and then in the quiet of his own room cried out in despair: "Oh, that I might know my own heart!"

The strenuousness of this desire is seen on the nineteenth of January, 1845. It is two o'clock Sabbath morning and in his small room, dark and cold and lonely, he has risen "to prepare by sober thought and prayer for the coming ordinance of the Lord's Supper."

Think what it meant to him! The solemn height of all his struggles gained at last! Remember what he had suffered and be not surprised that with this suffering as a background he should now have looked for the seal of his acceptance in an experience as bright as that was dark. Yet as he looked for spiritual ecstasy that morning and guided the pen through which he did his thinking, body and soul alike seemed cold. No rapture from heaven was sent him and he could not fly outside himself to find it. The wings of his soul seemed broken. He did not realize how imperative are physical laws nor how sadly even spiritual possibilities are limited by physical conditions. He was thinking, and praying, and writing when he needed sleep and rest. And because he did not understand why he lacked emotion we have this closing page of his early spiritual history : —

"In prayer since I arose I have had none of those drawings out of soul — going after Christ — which Christians so often speak of. I have none of that peace and joy which I hoped to have enjoyed. All seems cold and chill. I am surprised at myself.

"What! Am I about to commemorate the dying

love of a Redeemer, yet feel no emotion of love to that Redeemer? Feel no thankfulness to him from whom I hope I have received pardon? Oh! let me pray and meditate. I cannot go to the table of the Lord feeling thus. Would it not be sinful? I have thought I would renew my dedication to God, and put it in writing that it may make a deeper impression upon me. This dedication is nothing but the performance of my duty — that which I should do were I irretrievably doomed to hell. I am about to address my Maker. May I be suitably afraid and solemn!"

The self-dedication that follows is so long that only a small part of it can be quoted. But bear in mind that it was written at two o'clock in the morning by a boy of sixteen who was overshadowed by the awful thought that he deceived himself — that in spite of his aspiration and his hopes he was not a Christian.

The formality of the covenant and of the prayer that breathes through it is no doubt explained by the views of God which Halsey entertained, and by the religious reading he had done. We see that it was written for future reference : —

A DEDICATION OF MYSELF TO GOD.

"Eternal and unchangeable Jehovah; thou great Creator of heaven and earth, and adorable Lord of angels and men! I desire with the deepest humiliation and abasement of soul to fall down, at this time, in thine awful presence, and earnestly pray that thou wilt penetrate my very heart with a suitable sense of thine unutterable and inconceivable glories.

" ' Who am I, O Lord, or what is my house,' what is my nature or desert that I should speak of this, and desire that I may be one party in a covenant where thou, ' the King of kings, and Lord of lords,' art the other? But, O Lord, great as is thy majesty, so also is thy mercy. Behold, therefore, O Lord, I come unto thee. Receive, I beseech thee, thy poor revolted creature who desires nothing in the world so much as to be thine.

" Hear, O God of heaven, and record it in the book of thy remembrance, that henceforth I am thine, entirely thine. From this day do I solemnly renounce all the ' former lords ' which have had dominion over me, every sin and every desire, and bid in thy name an eternal defiance to the powers of hell. To thee do I consecrate all the remainder of my time upon earth, and beg that thou wouldst instruct and influence me, so that, whether my abode here be longer or shorter, every day and hour may be used in such a manner as shall most effectually promote thine honor and subserve the schemes of thy gracious providence.

" In this course, O blessed God, would I steadily persevere to the very end of my life; earnestly praying that every future day of it may supply the deficiencies and correct the irregularities of the former.

"I leave, O Lord, to thy management and direction all I possess and all I wish. Continue or remove what thou hast given me. Bestow or refuse what I imagine I want, as thou, Lord, shalt see good.

"Use me, O God, I beseech thee, as the instrument of thy glory, and honor me so far as, either by doing or suffering what thou shalt appoint, I may bring some revenue of praise to thee and benefit to the world in which I dwell. And when I have done and borne thy will upon earth, call me from hence at what time and in what manner thou pleasest. Only grant that in my dying moments, and in the near approach of eternity, I may remember these my engagements to thee, and may employ my latest breath in thy service.

"And do thou, O Lord, when thou seest the agonies of dissolving nature upon me, remember this covenant too, even though I should then be incapable of recollecting it. Look down then, O my heavenly Father, with a pitying eye upon thy languishing, thy dying child; place thine everlasting arms under me for support; put strength and confidence into my departing spirit, and receive it to the embrace of thine everlasting love.

"I desire to live and die as with my hand on that hope. Amen.   LUTHER HALSEY GULICK."
"January 19, 1845."

CHAPTER VIII.

MEDICAL STUDIES.

THROUGH 1846 and until the fall of 1847 Halsey took special studies with Dr. Schapps, of Amboy, New Jersey. These studies were in preparation for both collegiate and medical work; this combination being made early as a possible help to himself, for he was not strong; and the journal unconsciously reveals a touch of comic pathos in the union of conditions diametrically opposed to sound health with this strenuous preparation for a doctor's life. Determined as always to improve the time, and evidently having no counselor near to advise him, he rises early to study and studies late. Religious life and emotion grow cold, and his lamentation is: —

"I do not rise early enough — though I rise with the first dawn of day — to have sufficient time to perform my devotional duties in such a manner as I should. And I do not take time at another hour because in haste to begin studying."

Going to bed late, he still rises at any time between three and five, yet can understand neither the "irresistible drowsiness" that oppresses him nor the brain that "seems dull," nor his "undevotional frame of mind." Hours and moments grow increasingly precious, but he is "overcome with sleepiness," "unable to study," is "drowsy in church," and mourns that he "should so dishonor God in public." He questions whether he is not growing "lukewarm," "cold," and calls upon himself to "beware," to remember "the cloud of witnesses," "to press on in Christ's strength."

Dyspepsia troubles him. He passes through a course of strict dieting, but diminishes not his studies. He faints away, goes home ill, and grows discouraged. But the record reads: —

"Woke at two. French till six. Anatomy till twelve. Drawing till half-past four."

Over and over again there is similar account of study when sleep was what he needed. Indeed, these months were devoted to relentless study and to unwitting transgression of physical laws. Yet a growing consciousness of failing health was forced upon him; and at last, by peremptory medical command, he stopped studying and sought the motherly care of his ever-loving aunt Eliza, his mother's only sister.

Thus far Halsey had looked forward with unwavering expectation to a full collegiate course as preliminary to his professional studies. Now, however, the outlook is discouraging: —

"I can study no longer. Of course college will be

deferred another year. But by that time I think I may hope to enter the junior class." Though three months of farm life had helped him, and though studies were resumed in the fall, still he was far from well. And by the following spring the final decision was made: —

"Dr. Halsey says that, as I am, I could not sit down to a regular course of classical collegiate studies. Of course I acquiesce with the most perfect readiness. There is no use in attempting what one cannot do. So then, what will be the sum of my education will depend altogether or in great measure on my health. If I have health, I can study whatever is thought best; and it will make but little difference where I am to study if I can but have the books."

In view of the situation, Dr. Halsey advised in favor of a medical course first, and after that theological study, if health should then allow it. The result was that Halsey entered the New York College of Physicians and Surgeons in the fall of 1847.

And now, though medicine was his chosen profession, yet pulsing through all the record of his studies we feel the enthusiasm which was his in other lines of thought. The note he makes of outside reading in 1847 proves this: Campbell on Systematic Theology; Douglass on Missions; Kitto's Palestine; Life of Byron; Dr. Madden on Infirmities of Genius; Mason's

Ecclesiastical History; Taylor's Theory of Another Life; Lord Brougham's Statesmen; Shelley; Keats; Burns; Cambray on Eloquence; D'Israeli's Essays; Milman's Fall of Jerusalem; Fénélon on Eloquence; several of Shakespeare's plays; Life of Sir J. Reynolds; Hodge's Way of Life; Life of Gibbon; Foster on Decision of Character; Life of Dr. Arnold.

With this but a part of one year's reading, we can appreciate the fierce determination which was necessary to hold him to the work of medical study. Indeed, his own words testify to this. Recognizing the tendency but realizing present duty he says:—

"I am not a physician in my habit of mind. I must make myself so, whatever else I am. Medical subjects in their practical details must form much of my study. Medicine is my profession, in which I must perfect myself — medicine and theology primarily; natural science and composition secondarily for amusement."

Reaching around all other interests was his ever-growing absorbing enthusiasm for public speaking. Signs of this had appeared before. But now, in his young manhood, they were multiplied. Touches of ambition also came to him — a desire to reach people, to move them, to be felt and recognized as a force in their lives. To us who read it is as if a new element of character were suddenly introduced; as if a new adjustment of conditions were suddenly required. And Halsey, too, is perplexed. Is this burning, high ambition a part of the noble manhood he has longed for? Can it, too, find a place in the fabric of his consecrated life? His nineteenth birthday shows this perplexity, and with it the new adjustment.

"Here I sit with irresolution and prodigality of time; an itching after fame, a despicable one. Oh, had I a friend, I'd open my heart! My pen's my tongue, this page my friend. I cannot desire to be unknown. I envy the post of a Chalmers. I wish to acquire those qualities which will enable me to lead, while at the same time I wish to be led by piety and reverence, and implicit confidence in divine revelation."

At this point came opportunity to speak each Sabbath in a mission chapel on Fifty-first Street. He gladly accepted, and with clear self-knowledge quietly states again his own ambition with reference to public speaking: —

"The whole bent of my mind for years, I might say for almost my whole life, has been in this direction, and I still have strong predilections for it, stronger than for anything else."

Later he emphasizes the point: —

"The whole passion of my soul for many years has been to become a preacher. I feel confident of powers which, if properly directed, can secure me favorable attention."

Will powers be "properly directed" in a land where no audience appreciates, where no mind will understand him? Yet Halsey Gulick was moving toward heathenism so deep that neither audience nor thinkers were anywhere within it.

In the meantime, however, he goes to hear Mr. Forrest in Macbeth with the avowed purpose of studying eloquence. He buys a life of Whitefield and studies this also to learn the source of his power in public speaking. Then, best of all, he attends a course of six lectures on Shakespeare by Mr. Richard A. Dana, an event which he pronounces "the greatest intellectual treat I have enjoyed for a long time."

It may be that these lectures laid for him the foundation of that devotion to Shakespeare which was an enthusiasm always, a devotion which grew into an intimacy so close that in later years his children as little dreamed that his traveling outfit was complete without his well-worn Shakespeare as without the well-worn Bible.

During this time he found pleasant friends among Union Seminary theological students. "Men of choice spirit," he calls them; "men with whom I can feel and act." Yet though he had these friends, he often suffered from an intensity of depression which he accepted as an inevitable part of his life, his inheritance. Just what this depression was we are not told; but shadows which it cast prove its reality.

"I know I shall never be that jolly, laughing being many another one is, for I have such frequent returns of my constitutional depression of spirits as to prevent this. But if I may be useful, I shall be happy."

"I am alone. The possibilities of my future life oppress me, though I must acknowledge that I am now in one of my turns of low-spiritedness. These I have to make constant provision for. Oh, it is a source of relief to me to think of a coming stage of existence when I shall be relieved from these physical disabilities!"

This element of sadness does, indeed, thread itself through much of his recorded life. Due in part to physical conditions, and in greater part to his sensitive nature subjected to constant overwork, the resulting mental suffering is none the less real to him. But he learns to accept himself as he is, and in 1849 is pleased because he "begins to see the boy gradually wearing off," because "the fermentation of youth is subsiding." Yet, since the beginning, the world and his journal have seen wondrous little of the boy in this serious-minded youth.

Side by side with these touches of pain, with the record of lectures attended, books read and efforts made for earning money, are constant spirited notes of news from Europe, from California, from the world. And as a background to the devotion with which he still consecrated himself to foreign missionary work there is touching significance in the throbbing interest with which he thus watched the movement of the nations. He was keenly alive to each flash of news that came; the more so perhaps as the months in hurrying by forced him relentlessly toward the point where suddenly he should drop out of all this life and action, and on some lonely island should wait for news that could only reach him once a year — that might, indeed, not reach him even then.

Now, however, he is part of this intensity, and his journals alone would introduce one fairly to the great events of these years. We watch Austria and Germany in 1848, and the French Republic as she elects her president. We follow the Pope in his hegira from Rome, and realize the wild enthusiasm with which the discovery of gold in California is greeted, and the indignation of the country over a supposed secret codicil to our treaty with Mexico.

Items from the whole mission world also steal their way into these pages, while quiet comments of approval and disapproval demonstrate already the calm strength of the growing mind and the depth of his interest in all missionary problems. What else was, indeed, to be expected? For now, as in the beginning, the compass of his own life pointed unswervingly to missionary work, to work for others, for the most needy wherever they might be. Years before he had written: —

"I cannot now conceive of anything, if life and health are spared, that will deter me from becoming a foreign missionary. In accordance with this purpose I am determined nothing shall be allowed to pass unimproved which shall render me more useful." And this thought dominated the years.

Already we have found him speaking each Sabbath on Fifty-first Street. Later he helped organize a Sunday-school in the same place; and recognizing the unity of all work for others, he at once sees the world's noble mission field stretched out before him. Its door is open. He stands upon the threshold.

"Thus do I begin my missionary life. I hope it will not cease till life itself ceases. I am a missionary now as much as I ever shall be. A habit of doing good neglected now will never be perfectly formed."

Uniting this home work to foreign fields was the meeting of the American Board in Pittsfield, Mass., in 1849. Here Halsey listened with quiet discrimination to those who had toiled on the field and to those who, at home, had theorized. Here too he met again young people from Hawaii, playmates once, fellow students now in New England. With Hiram Bingham he walked to Chester. With Warren Chamberlain he climbed Mount Holyoke, and, seated there above the world, these two young men looked out on life as seriously as they studied the picture before them. They "talked of youthful days and future prospects." Then, with the past of childhood behind them and the future of life rising high before them, they knelt and prayed there on the mountain.

Thenceforward, boys who had inspired one another in their Honolulu spelling school became a larger inspiration to each other. Halsey Gulick and Sereno Bishop and Hiram Bingham, schoolmates then, are correspondents now. And Halsey's letters, prized and kept through many years, are before us to-day. Each carries its message. Each touches, through query or exclamation, the keynote of his life; and all ring as earnestly to-day as they sounded forty years ago when they were written. Even now he pleads for Polynesia:

"Fellow Polynesians, we are bound by double ties of fellowship. And shall we not be brought under a third bond of unity by engagement in the same life of evangelization of Polynesia?"

Indeed, through journals and through letters, we increasingly realize that the unshaken, ever-strengthening purpose of his life was to be a missionary to Polynesia.

"The elevation of Polynesia! For this I will live, for this die. It is but my duty. It will be my pleasure. I may not do much. I may not have the capacity. I may not be allowed the length of life. But to do all I can, whether much or little, is my obligation and my aim; the elevation politically, socially, intellectually, religiously, the last accomplished securing the rest; therefore it shall be my main endeavor."

With this goal before him, Halsey bent every energy to its attainment, and on the ninth of March, 1850, he was graduated in medicine, and took what he terms the "solemn, imperative oath."[1]

Thus another milestone of life was passed; and soberly facing the future, he wondered where the next would find him.

---

[1] For the sake of lessened expense he had previously transferred his connection from the College of Physicians and Surgeons to the University of New York.

CHAPTER IX.

FINAL PREPARATIONS.

DURING his three years of medical study Halsey had attended various courses of lectures in Union Theological Seminary, where Dr. Halsey was at the time lecturing on ecclesiastical history. Much of his reading had also been in theological directions, and now he planned to begin systematic theological study. This was also Dr. Halsey's advice.

Just here it is interesting to know of an offer of help made to and promptly refused by him because it involved pledged allegiance to Princeton theology. He makes this vigorous statement of the case to his parents:—

"If I go to a seminary at all, as go I will if I can, I go to examine these subjects of dispute. Mr. D., who last fall offered to do much for me at Princeton, told me they did not want any one who could not act cordially with them and who would prove recreant to Old Schoolism. But for this I should now be preparing to enter Princeton Seminary. It is more than I ever will do — to constrain myself to think in any prescribed way. If facts carefully thought over bring me to the creed of my ancestors, all is well, and I will profess it; if not, not. I have bid myself act as my instructors have taught me until such time as I can examine the subjects carefully for myself.

"I am a Protestant by education, and I have so far imbibed its principles as to refuse to admit into my religious faith any article I have not fully and independently examined. As to Old and New Schoolism, I do not know which I shall be; indeed, I am sure I shall not allow myself to be involved in the disputes of a past decade. On this I am resolved: if receiving help from any source requires of me that I think no otherwise than as the benefactors think, I shall promptly decline their benefaction. This I have done in reference to Mr. D."

At this point, however, an important crisis in Hawaiian mission history changed the course of Halsey Gulick's life.

During the summer of 1850 he learned that a mission to some of the Micronesian Islands had been projected and that the Hawaiian Island Mission was to act upon it the following May. In view of this he was greatly moved. Through it he saw the possible accomplishment of his most cherished desire — "A Hawaiian mission with Hawaiian missionaries, of whom I should like to be one!" But opposing this there stood his other great hope for theological study, for preparation for the life of a preacher. We imagine the strait 'twixt two in which he was placed, and we speculate as to influences which will weigh in the balance and determine the future for him.

On the one hand was love of study and hope for greater usefulness through greater preparation; on the other was the fact of a medical profession already entered upon and an immediate call to work in the field to which, through solemn dedication, he had already given himself. In his perplexity he consulted Dr. Anderson, then Foreign Secretary of the American Board, and received advice against the added theological course, in favor of an early return to the Pacific, and in recommendation of an immediate application for appointment by the Board. Solemn advice for the older man to give to the younger, but conscientiously given, and with this thrown into the scales the weight on that side was heavier.

Of himself alone was he now in doubt. "Am I ready?" But the hesitation did not last. "I am about decided to offer myself. Divine wisdom will, I hope, direct and control me." Then with the exultation of self-conquest, with the memory of parental example shining around him, with a thrill in his voice, he adds: "Father, it is your own son who wishes to go to the heathen. Why should I withhold myself for the luxury of a few more years of study?"

And so the decision was bravely made and the formal offer of himself to the Board followed it.

In view of his passion for books, his burning desire to be a preacher, and his incompleted course of study, we instinctively look for expressed regret or, at least, for some paragraph that shall distinctly speak of these shattered hopes as a sacrifice to duty; but he does not write of any disappointment. The steps before him had seemed clearly marked, and he took them quietly and firmly, making no lamentation because of others which might have been pleasanter; he only says: —

"Oh, I stand curious at the close of each day to know what the next shall reveal of divine mercy and wisdom! It is a pleasure to trace the thread of divine plan which seems to run through my actions during the past year. I knew not the plan I was developing till now I see it in retrospection, and it is under this impression that I step forward cheerfully to meet the ever-coming future. I only see the few stepping-stones that are just before me in the dashing flood. I trust a Father's hand to direct my general course. I may die before the year expires, but this will, I hope, only hasten my emancipation from this defective body I am in. It will not check my happiness nor my usefulness, only perfect both."

Then the official appointment came to "a new

mission which it is in contemplation to fit out from the Hawaiian Islands to some other group in the Pacific Ocean."

But Halsey Gulick, Dr. Gulick now, was not to sail for almost a year yet. He spent this year — 1851 — in hospital practice in New York, in further study of Greek and Hebrew, in attending lectures, and in still continued indefatigable reading.

During this year, also, he transferred his connection from the Presbyterian church on Houston Street to the Broadway Tabernacle, where Rev. J. P. Thompson was pastor. The reasons for the change were very plain to himself as he traced them, and quite as plain to us who follow now : —

"I do this because in my future foreign missionary life I shall probably prefer and, indeed, be under the necessity of acting with my fellow missionaries on the Congregational basis ; and I should prefer becoming a little accustomed to it here. Furthermore, there is such occasional stress laid on the minutiæ of the Calvinistic system by the different bodies of the Presbyterian body that I rebel. I do not wish to feel myself as liable to the authoritative whims of weak-minded men. As I seem to see the usual tenor of Presbyterianism about me, it is representative but in form, in name. And authority is exercised over thinking in a way I dislike. For myself I prefer thinking freely, without alarm lest I think heterodoxy. Yet I shall look back with fondness to those examples of mild, patriarchal discipline by fathers and elders, which I shall ever regard as the beau-ideal of government."

Later, in conversation with Dr. Thompson, he was advised to ask not only for license before he sailed for Micronesia, but for ordination as well. And we share with him the sense of exaltation which this anticipated, authorized place in the wider field would give him. To be recognized by the Church as worthy to speak publicly and work for Christ! To be not only licensed but ordained! This was more than he had dared to hope for. Yet it had come to him unsought. And with thankfulness in his heart he exclaims: —

"Thus is my way opened, and I may hope to have the prominent plan of my life accomplished."

Then a council was called by the Broadway Tabernacle. Among those present as delegates were Rev. William Patton, Rev. George B. Cheever, Rev. H. O. Schermerhorn, Rev. R. S. Storrs, Rev. Timothy Atkinson, and Rev. J. P. Thompson. Dr. Patton was chosen moderator, and Dr. Cheever was the scribe. By these men, some of them in their prime, some of them still young with all the glory of life before them, Dr. Gulick was examined and accepted as a fellow worker. This was on the fourth of October, 1851.

FINAL PREPARATIONS.

On the evening of the 5th, Sabbath evening, the consummation of all his preparation was reached. A large congregation had gathered in the Broadway Tabernacle, and kneeling for ordination, while the hands of good men rested on him, Dr. Gulick felt that he was crowned. Again he prayed; and again he consecrated himself to the loneliness of Micronesia and to any work that God should give him anywhere.

Before he sailed, however, still another great event was to widen his life and add increasing impetus to its natural currents. This was his marriage.

Perhaps his nearest previous approach to love was a breathing of romance which came to him one summer when he was eighteen. And though, as compared to that experience, he at the time pronounced "romance but a shadow, poetry but a well-touched picture," still it came to an end. To comfort himself he assured his journal with philosophic calm that "though it is painful, the pains are those attending a necessary amputation."

In this connection various other items are full of significance. Once it is in reply to a letter from his mother: —

"I sometimes love to read of those good old days when Abraham could say to his 'eldest servant': 'Go unto my country, and to my kindred, and take a wife unto my son Isaac.' No troublesome courtships then

— all done by proxy. Aye; and those were the days of Rebekahs and Rachels. But hold — Rachel? No proxy there, I am sure. Am I a Jacob, and have I to work for my own wife? May it not be a seven years' service! So with a laugh and a prayer I dismiss the subject, which, by the way, is a fair exhibition of my feelings. I know the pleasure; I dread the difficulty; I fear the result; and so most earnestly desire the favor of the Lord."

A later comment reads: "As for courtship, woe is me! I can never consent to waste my time!"

But after all, the human heart remained and its human requirement. That era passed, and serious thoughts came to him of a possible life companion.

"My heart is full of emotion which I may not or cannot express. Oh for the time when I may have a friend to whom I may tell all!"

But he was not very sanguine, and one day there is dejection in his journal: —

"Brainerd had no wife. Henry Martyn had no wife. Schwartz had no wife. Vanderkemp had no wife, when he went out. Fisk had no wife. Parsons had no wife. Why need I be alarmed if I am to have none?"

Then he passed through a season of what he terms "haggard expectancy," but closes it with a hallelujah:

"Joy and devout thankfulness are mine! Miss

Louisa Lewis has yielded her assent, and consents to live with me and be my friend for life and my fellow missionary."

Each day he grew happier, till, on the twenty-third of October, he writes: —

"Joys accumulate! Happiness floods my soul! What shall I render to the Lord for all his benefits! Next week Wednesday I am to be married to her who I think has been appointed for me and for whom I was appointed. May the blessing of the Lord guide and accompany us ever, securing the constant continuance of that endearment and pleasure we now experience!"

The following week brought the wedding day with its emphasized happiness. And on the 30th are the happiest words in all these journal pages: —

"Yesterday I was married to Miss Louisa Lewis! I am happy! I AM HAPPY! There does not remain an important wish ungratified. I am in the fruition of all that earth can render me. My only anxiety comes from imagining that such joy cannot be expected long to continue. Yet saddening providences will not destroy our happiness. No, naught but sin can, and against it we pray. We are husband and wife. We are fellow Christians. We are fellow missionaries, and we pray for blessing on each aspect of our lives."

Louisa Lewis, now Mrs. Gulick, was born in New

York city on the tenth of November, 1830. Her grandfather, Robert Wardell, was one of the early dry-goods merchants of Wall Street. In his childhood, Canal Street, a canal then in the suburbs of the city, was his skating ground. Louisa[1] was the oldest daughter in the family of four sisters and one brother. In her childhood she had been familiarized with the thought of foreign missions by some neighbors who had returned from India — the first generation of the missionary family of Scudders.

After studies carried on in Rutgers Seminary, New York city, and two winters of teaching in North Carolina, Louisa had for months before her marriage been engaged with her mother in city missionary work in New York. Her devotion to work for others and her forgetfulness of self had been marked characteristics since she was a child; and when this new opening came for a larger work in a darker place she saw at once the guiding hand of God and was ready to be led.

A printed account appearing at the time gives a word about the wedding and testifies to what Mrs. Gulick already was to those who knew her: —

"Whether Dr. Gulick's wife knows fully what she

---

[1] Louisa's father, Junius Sidney Lewis, was gifted in conversation, brilliant in repartee, whole-souled, full of life and enterprise, a helpful Christian merchant. Her mother, Sarah Wardell Lewis, had been delicately nurtured, and was active always in Christian work.

has undertaken is a little doubtful; yet she is not one likely to be disheartened or to shrink from danger. In the time of the cholera she was a ministering angel to many a suffering and dying family. She went from house to house of *the poor*, where aid is most needed and most scantily given, and offered her assistance with no regard for the danger to herself. Such a woman is likely to do good wherever she may go."

Then follows the query which so often meets this sort of self-sacrifice: —

"Isn't it a little singular that persons who are remarkable not so much for physical adaptation as for intellectual superiority and real gentleness of soul, should so often be the ones to devote themselves to raising up tribes and nations where the human mind is an utter blank and desolation?"

And picturing what the new life and surroundings must mean to this young couple, the writer breathes a prayer which we unconsciously make our own: —

"May the sun's rays fall gently on their island home, and as they shut out the world from their hopes may they be more than the world to each other!"

As we have seen, Dr. and Mrs. Gulick were married on the twenty-ninth of October, 1851. Mrs. Gulick was almost twenty-one, her husband twenty-three, years old. On the eighteenth of November they sailed from Boston for the Hawaiian Islands. Friends were there to say "Farewell" and "God speed you." To each it seemed a separation for life, Micronesia was so far away.

As the young couple stand on the deck of the small craft, we see fulfilled at last the semi-prophetic yearning of years before when, longing for Martin Luther's opportunity, Luther Halsey Gulick had written: "But those days are passed, and I must prepare for usefulness in some other sphere, though it may be I shall yet have opportunity to ascertain what spirit I am of."

And has not the opportunity come to him now?

CHAPTER X.

FAREWELL.

THIS company of missionaries was the last which the Board sent to the Pacific via Cape Horn. It included ten persons, six returning to the Hawaiian Islands, and four, Mr. and Mrs. Snow and Dr. and Mrs. Gulick, pioneers facing Micronesia.

The Esther May was small, her cabin full, and to accommodate all the passengers an added room was fitted up below deck. This was separated by a suspended sheet from the cargo of the bark. The proximity of sails, ropes, tar, barrels of fish, and barrels of pork was not an æsthetic inspiration to seasick passengers. Indeed, this sheet failed in various ways as a nonconductor, for sounds of scurrying mice, no less than scent of fish, and flesh, and tar, were clearly apprehended through it.

Nor was the slender, swaying white partition — white at first — much protection during their first storm. When it overtook them tumultuous waves poured over the narrow deck and down the hatchways; cargo and cabin alike were flooded; all loose articles floated about in the harmony of rhythmic motion, while miniature waves within the cabin dashed in unison with monster waves without.

Doubtless the missionaries appreciated the comedy no less than the tragedy of the situation. But tragedy must have waxed and comedy waned when, for thirty-six hours, they were calked down in their cabin of small dimensions, while noise and darkness, and cargo that tossed about, were their only companions; while sailors stood with axes ready to cut away the masts, and death faced them every moment.

From the midst of trunks filled with water and boxes of books hopelessly soaked, Dr. Gulick no doubt recalled with grim appreciation the anxiety of a secretary in Boston that discipline be secured to the youthful missionary. He had asked permission to go to Hawaii via Panama, the newly opened route involving a journey of sixty-five days, and the answer from the older man to the younger was dignified and solemn: "My young brother," he said, "a foreign missionary needs the discipline of a voyage around Cape Horn." For discipline, therefore, missionary devotion to Micronesia was spending five months instead of two upon the water. And though reading and study filled the weeks,[1] time passed slowly.

---

[1] In this line a summary at its close shows what Dr. Gulick accomplished during the voyage. Daily readings in Hebrew, Greek, and Hawaiian; some study of French; besides this, Stackhouse's History of the Bible, Latham on the Variety of the Races of Man, Mariner's

At last, however, land was before them. They were nearing the beautiful *Aina hanau*, the homeland left so long ago. In the distance, against skies more blue than skies have ever seemed since these last swept above him, Dr. Gulick sees again the hazy outline of far-off mountains. For hours these float as airy tents above the clouds that hold them. Then their outline grows a trifle clearer. Land is seen below them; clouds are traced across them; and gradually from the gray there evolve the softest shades of green. As the tint grows deeper the long coastline is plainly seen; while dashing over sands white and bleached by myriad washings is the surf that rolls and foams and breaks, and with a sweeping caress is lost for a moment, then, slowly turning back, prepares to come again. Sight of it all came first, and then the sound, the musical ripple and swish and roar of waters in constant motion. Twelve years before a tone of utter sadness mingled with the music of their movement, but to-day who can measure all the gladness that it brings!

They passed the beautiful islands one by one and were anchored, at last, two miles from Honolulu. It

---

Tongo Islands, Life in Fiji, Morell's History of Modern Philosophy, Edwards on Revivals, on Original Sin, on the Affections, and on Faith, Chalmer's Memoir and Sermons. In addition, **four sermons written and two outlined**. And all this accomplished in spite of the fact that a sea voyage was for him "a constant intellectual misery."

was March 24, 1852, Sabbath day; and here they waited for Monday morning.

Years of separation lay behind Dr. Gulick and his friends; there were but two miles of quiet water between them now; and yet, because of their sturdy loyalty to what they thought was meant by "Remember the Sabbath day to keep it holy," parents and brothers spent the day on shore, while Dr. Gulick and his wife still tarried on the Esther May.

Dr. Gulick was twelve when he left. On his return he was twenty-three. Had time and distance banished him from the lives of his younger brothers? What else was possible? And yet, if written thoughts ever take the place of spoken words; if molded lives are ever any proof of personal influence, — we know that he did not return as a stranger to his home. Indeed, he was so good a friend that his written desires for himself had unconsciously set the standard for his brothers. They instinctively felt that thus in turn must they strive; that his high goal must be their goal too. He had over and over again assumed their unity of purpose.

"It cannot be," he had written, "that seven boys were sent here just to take up room and eat food and wear out clothes. I don't believe it. . . . Let us be an earnest family in mind and heart, and do much for the world of thought and religion. We can if we but will. . . . Let not our family history be that of sightless worms, boring the mud for bare existence. . . . An author is judged by his books, a mechanic by his machines, and a parent by his children. Are not at least John, Charles, Theodore, and Thomas to be missionaries?"

From boyhood to manhood he had thus come to them constantly as a mental and a moral inspiration. And it would be difficult, perhaps, to measure the effect of his written words on the lives of his six brothers. In truth, the voice which for years had called to them across the ocean was strengthened for them by the mystery of distance and America, academy and university which lay behind it. Year by year it had formed part of their growing life. It had emphasized the daily petition of their father that his children might " have the glorious privilege of preaching the gospel to the heathen."

With such preparation it is not strange that in time this privilege came to each in turn. Now, however, they were still young. Their Joseph had returned a great man, with a wife and a commission to preach that "glorious gospel" to yet more heathen islands. Orramel had seen him, and Charles, who was now in America; but to the younger boys and to his sister Halsey stepped off the Esther May to greet them at once a brother and a hero.

It is not quite possible to picture the meeting again after the long separation, nor to show all the change which Dr. Gulick found among his friends.

This aged man who greets them is his father, gray twelve years ago, snowy white to-day; and this, his mother, more bent and tired now, but with eyes as brown and bright and full of tears as when he left her. Such different tears to-day! And this band of boys crowded close about him are his brothers, changed in limb and face and clothing, but unchanged of heart, welcoming in boyish fashion their brother — their hero — and the new sister that he brings. Last of all, like trailing arbutus among them, is the shy little sister with her Madonna face, the sister he had never seen before.

And this was home again! This its inner circle! But other circles were no less changed. Friends of all ages had taken the same forward step. For the nation itself, for its Christianity and its civilization, the step seemed longest.

Even now but thirty-two years had passed since the first missionary landed, and this is what we find: — a population of eighty-four thousand Hawaiians,[1] a form of government changed from the unmeasured tyranny of the Tabu system to a limited monarchy, a house of hereditary nobles and representatives

[1] The deaths for 1850 were 4,330; the births 1,422.

chosen by the people, churches and schools scattered from Hawaii to Niihau, an annual government allowance to its common schools of $26,000, and in these schools fifteen thousand pupils. In fact, schools and scholars of all ages were so multiplied that knowledge of reading and writing, geography, bookkeeping, history, and theology were claimed to outstrip all mechanical attainments. In addition to all else there was a church membership of twenty-one thousand; three ordained pastors, and a Christian community so large that a missionary remarks without even an exclamation point: "Some of our prisons are nearly destitute of inmates, and the district judges complain for want of something to do."

Anticipating the mission to Micronesia, the Hawaiian Missionary Society had been formed in 1851 as auxiliary to the American Board. Its contribution the first year was $6,140.

Hawaiian history had now fairly entered upon a new era. Heretofore Christian life had grown by what it received; hereafter it was to grow by what it gave. The importance of this step to Hawaiian church life cannot be overestimated. Ultimately designed for those in lower estate than they were, it was nevertheless taken primarily for the benefit of the Hawaiians themselves. They had reached that point in progressive Christianity where work for others was needed to sustain and animate the home life.

As of all new enterprises, so of this there had been question. Even now it was difficult, nay, in certain cases wellnigh impossible, to maintain self-supporting churches. Why then organize a new work which would require yet larger giving? Does not charity begin at home? On the whole, however, there had been union of conviction. The society had been organized. While interest slowly grew in a possible mission of their own, and while funds were coming in to help them begin it, the missionaries for that field had made the journey. They had arrived at last, and stood expectant and questioning on Hawaiian soil. Would these churches feel ready seriously to attempt all that was involved in this proposed foreign mission?

The answer to the question is found in the events of the succeeding four months.

With the coming of the Esther May, what was growing interest before mounted rapidly to glowing enthusiasm. With The Missionary Herald and letters before us, it is easy to live over again those four months of history; to watch the onward movement of its missionary wave, and to appreciate the increasing momentum with which it rose to rapid culmination in the sailing of the Caroline.

Preliminary work had already been done, and when

the Esther May came, bringing with her a child of their own land — a young man clear-eyed and brave, — eager to be their missionary to Micronesia, playmates of other days and Hawaiians everywhere recognized and welcomed him as their standard-bearer.

Dr. Gulick was soon speaking in Hawaiian. Mr. Snow was no less earnest through an interpreter, while older missionaries and native Christians were all successfully working for the same object — the increase of mission interest among the people. The speaking and the praying were but the fanning of the flame. There was soon no question as to the will of the churches.

Of interest now there was no lack. Money they had generously given and prayers were daily offered. But what of that more serious proposition? Were men and women ready to make the larger gift? Who would go as the first Hawaiian missionary to foreign lands? This was the most serious question ever yet submitted to the Hawaiian churches. And missionary fathers of the Christian life of Hawaii must have held their breath till the answer came, for it would prove, as nothing else, how deep the roots of Christian life had reached. But the question was hardly asked before it was answered, first by one, then by another, until seven couples stood as candidates asking for liberty to go.

From among these seven two alone were to be chosen; not by lot, as Matthias, but by careful deliberation. And while the people prayed about it, and while the candidates were willing to go or to stay, as should be judged best, the annual meeting of the mission was held in Honolulu. It continued in session from May 6 to June 4. By formal action it passed the responsibility of the Micronesian Mission into the hands of the Hawaiian Missionary Society; and from among the seven waiting candidates two were finally chosen — Daniela Opunui, a school-teacher in the prime of life, a graduate of Lahainaluna Seminary, and Doreka, his wife; and Berita Kaaikaula, a deacon, the owner of some property, the father of two children, and Deborah, his wife. Both children were left in Honolulu when the parents sailed for Micronesia.

With the missionary society formed, the missionaries chosen, and the field waiting for them nearly three thousand miles away, the pressing question was as to the wisest move first to be made. Of the field itself little was known. Sea captains "would not give a straw," they said, "for the lives of men and women who should attempt to live in Micronesia." Still missionary purpose did not swerve. It was suggested that, for safety, the husbands go first to "spy out the land" and come again for their wives. But separation seemed impossible when so much was involved, and all decided to go together.

A further question was as to the vessel they should take; and this too was promptly answered, for generous Hawaiian love, putting its arms still more closely about its foreign mission, bought for it the schooner Caroline.

With each new decision larger interest was secured. Natives and foreigners were unitedly enlisted in practical zeal. The children of the missionaries, many of them young men and women, united as the "Hawaiian Mission Children's Society" and pledged themselves to the support of Dr. Gulick and his wife. Lahainaluna Seminary held itself equally responsible for the salary of its graduate Opunui, and the Second Church of Honolulu assumed the support of Kaaikaula, its deacon.

The missionary meeting came to an end. The weeks were hurrying by. With so much of intensity in home life and in public life too, Dr. Gulick's journal was not often written. Yet in the midst of it, on the tenth of June, there is a significant birthday note: —

"Twenty-four years old to-day, and I am launched on the wide, wild sea of life."

The closing weeks were crowded with meetings and all were full of interest. But most impressive, perhaps, was that which included the public consecration of Messrs. Opunui and Kaaikaula with their wives to mission service. All were members of the Second Hawaiian Church of Honolulu.

It was the last Sabbath in June, and a thousand communicants were present that day. After celebrating the Lord's Supper together the Hawaiians about to leave spoke to their fellow Christians who were to stay and pray for them. And while they still stood, their wives standing with them, they received both charge and instruction from their pastor.[1] Then, to prove his people no less than to strengthen those who left them, Mr. Smith asked all to rise who were resolved to follow their missionaries " with prayer and contributions year after year, even until death" should come to them. There was no hesitation, for dusky Hawaiians are as easily moved by sacrifice and devotion as any other people. With one accord they rose to their feet, and standing for a moment they pledged themselves to changeless love for Micronesia and for the workers there.

Mr. and Mrs. Sturges had now arrived from the United States. They too were going to Micronesia.

On the sixth of July a council was called to organize the "Mission Church of Micronesia," the child of that other "Mission Church" organized

[1] Rev. Lowell Smith.

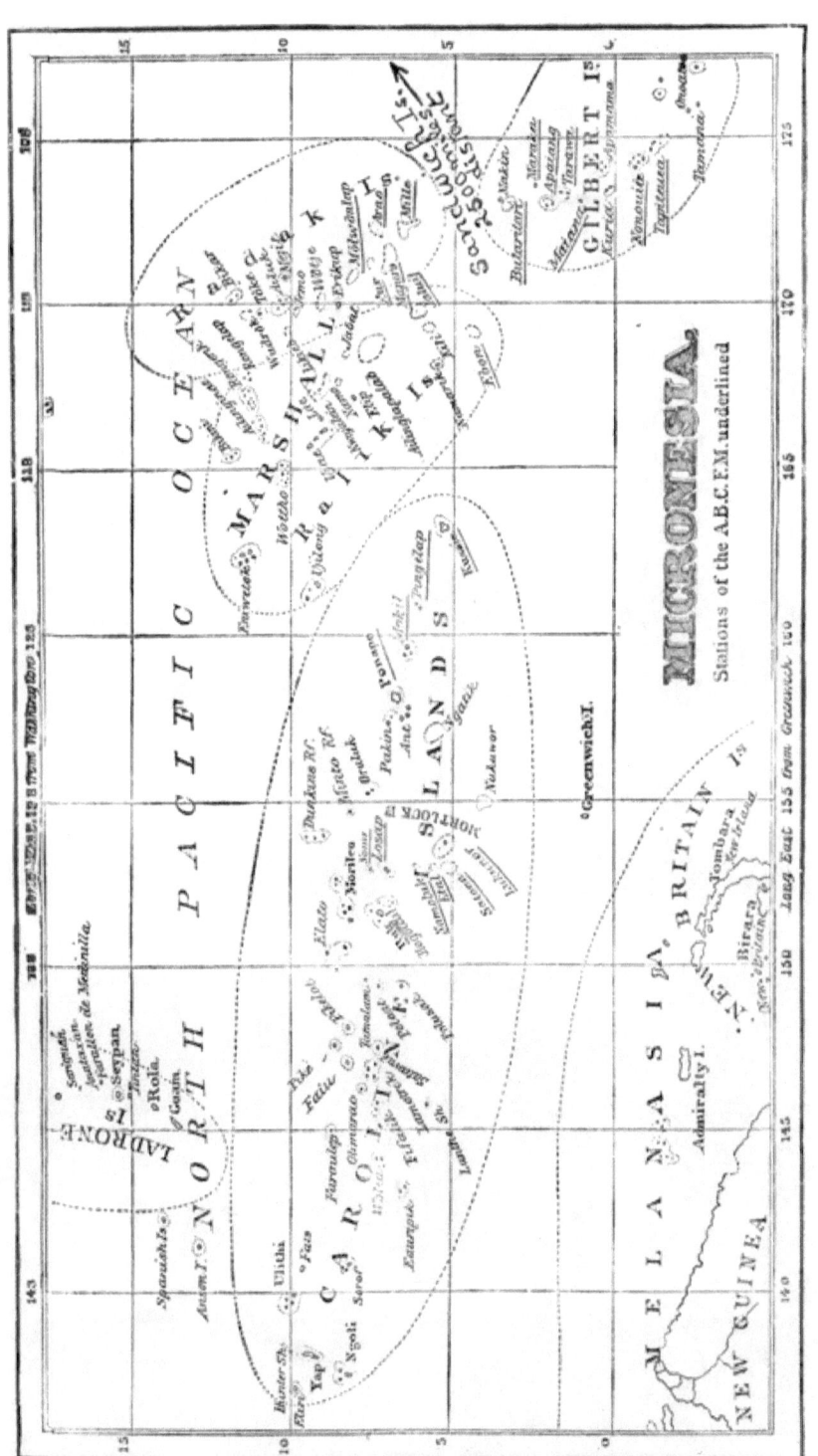

thirty-three years before in Park Street Church, Boston — the "Mission Church of the Hawaiian Islands." Of this newest church there were but ten members, five men and five women. A small force surely, yet a lever that should lift all Micronesia!

Friends now sent gifts of every sort: food for the voyage, comforts for the new life, letters to cheer them. In truth, the zeal for giving laid hold upon all, high and low, rich and poor, saint and sinner too, so it seems, for they say: "It is the wish of all, the wicked as well as the good, that the Lord may open wide the door before you."

Even royalty was stirred. With what touching readiness do those who have suffered try to help those who are still in pain! Anxious to do his part, Kamehameha III wrote a letter in Hawaiian to "all chiefs of the islands of this great ocean to the westward." To them he sent his "greetings" and his wish for them of "peace and happiness now and forever." And then he adds:—

"Here is my friendly message to you: There are about to sail for your islands some teachers of the Most High God Jehovah, to make known unto you his word for your eternal salvation. A part of them are white men from the United States of America and a part of them belong to my islands.

"I therefore take the liberty to commend these

good teachers to your care and friendship, to exhort you to listen to their instructions and to seek their acquaintance. I have seen the value of such teachers. . . . Many of my people regard the Word of God, Jehovah, and pray to him; and he has greatly blessed us. I advise you to throw away your idols, take the Lord Jehovah for your God, worship and love him, and he will bless and save you. May he make these new teachers a great blessing to you and your people and withhold from you no good thing!

"Камеhамеhа."

And now the Caroline is to sail. It is four o'clock in the afternoon, July 15, 1852 — a quiet, summer afternoon under a tropic sky. From the last prayer meeting in Honolulu missionaries and friends have come to the wharf. Hundreds are already there; Hawaiians in bright-colored, simple gowns, decked, as always, with wreaths of beautiful flowers, and missionaries in their sober costume; children are curious and excited and strangers are filled with astonishment. Natives and foreigners, old and young, all alike have eager faces. Some are tearful, others joyful. Some see only the heroism before them, others see only its pathos; but all realize that a new era has dawned for Hawaii.

Kaaikaula and Deborah are saying good-by to their

children. Dr. Gulick is once more saying "Good-by" — God be with you — to his mother. His wife is near him, his brothers, his sister, and his father; but his mother's heart aches most!

All who go are gathered upon the deck of the Caroline. The last moments have come; a hush has fallen; bowed heads are uncovered; heaven seems very near, and the cloud of witnesses close about them. Prayers are offered in English and Hawaiian. Then, as a fervent Amen to the praying, the giving, and the hoping, hundreds of voices join in singing: —

> "Waft, waft, ye winds, his story,
> And you, ye waters, roll,
> Till like a sea of glory
> It spreads from pole to pole."

After this the Caroline moved away. And while from deck and wharf friends still watched each other through the gloaming, darkness came between them and their watching was ended; yet they felt that God could still be reached. And rising to heaven from Hawaiian homes that night ten thousand prayers brushed the sails of the Caroline and wafted her on her way.

CHAPTER XI.

HAWAII TO KUSAIE.

TWENTY-FOUR people were on the Caroline: three foreign and two Hawaiian missionaries with their wives, Mr. Clark and Mr. Kekela, delegates from Hawaii to return again, and Mr. John Gulick, who accompanied his brother for the voyage. The rest were captain, crew, steward, and cook; thirteen passengers and a crew of eleven on a schooner of one hundred tons pressing toward Micronesia three thousand miles away!

If a photograph would do it, how easy to emphasize the smallness of the Caroline by placing beside it the ocean steamer that crosses the Atlantic to-day! Ten thousand tons tower broad and high against one hundred, and the difference in size is more than equaled by all the comfort that the smaller vessel lacked. Even to a zealous secretary in Boston the Esther May had seemed small enough and uncomfortable enough for needed missionary discipline; but the Esther May represented luxury itself as compared to the limited quarters of the Caroline. Its passengers were so crowded now that they had no staterooms;

so cramped that the table on which they dined was placed outside the cabin; while the service of the schooner was so inefficient that seasick missionary wives supervised the kitchen, washed and baked, and tried to be cheerful.

Twenty days of rain and sunshine were marked by irregular progress and adjustment to the constant nearness of each other. Then, on the fifth of August, land appeared, the most northern of the Gilbert Islands, a low shadow on the horizon; darker, more stable than a cloud, and far more real than cloudland to eager eyes that saw for the first time a Micronesian coral reef.

A line of trees and a beach of gleaming sand — that was all. No spot on that low-lying island was so high as the deck on which they stood, and they wondered whether men's thoughts could ever soar from so low an earthly spot to heaven that reached so high above them. Yet prayers that day rose straight and swift from the Caroline, and those who prayed thought an answer came as swiftly down. They prayed for an interpreter and they prayed for a welcome. Both came promptly to them. The natives proved friendly, amused and interested rather than hostile; the interpreter was an Englishman, who under his flying British ensign was a trader there in cocoanut oil.

Commerce had, indeed, years before sent its messengers to Micronesia, yet in spite of commerce with Christian lands not a ray of Christianity or of civilization had yet touched Butaritari. A thousand pardons of the shirts and the pipes! Yes; civilization had sometimes gasped in a flannel shirt under the burning sky, and it had laid its fiery hand on heathenism already in condition sad enough. Civilization had taught the native the art of liquor-making. It had refined the art of murder by supplying guns to hands that really wanted to kill. It had proved to the simple that the greater wisdom of the white man who came among them was shown in loving himself much more than he loved his neighbor.

The lesson had been learned, and now other white men had come; the same in kind, of course, for all arrive in ships, all have pale faces, all speak a barbarous tongue. But these other beings who came with them were surprising. "Women," the trader called them, "foreign women," and natives were astonished. How droll, how unnatural, how unfashionable they were! How disfigured, poor things! The heathen women were convulsed, nor did they conceal their amusement more than we do ours from monkeys and infants that please us. They followed them in companies; they gave them cocoanuts to eat and cocoanut milk to drink; they shook hands as an added joke, and had a merry time.

All were not, however, thus affected, only the frivolous, perhaps, for many were coolly indifferent, masters of staid self-possession. Yet all these inhabitants of Butaritari were interesting; large men, often six feet tall, and small women, brown skin for all and black eyes, long black hair, tattooing that theoretically supplied all deficiencies in costume, and cocoanut oil from head to foot — a shining mantle.

The garment worn was a pandanus leaf skirt about the waist. As a foreign touch a shirt was sometimes added, a hat also in the case of royalty. This the missionaries discovered when an interview was granted with the king. Mr. Randall, the trader, went with them. The palace was a low-spreading, straw-thatched roof, open on all sides, resting on posts four feet high, and covering ground enough to seat five hundred people — to seat them on its natural floor of sand and bits of jagged coral.

The throne was in the center of this building and the king upon it. All was most harmonious, for the throne was a simple platform, six feet square, raised a foot from the ground, and the king a lad of fourteen, whose royal attire, itemized by Mrs. Gulick, was a " soiled calico shirt, coarse pantaloons, and a straw hat, which he kept on through our visit."

Five hundred chiefs and people were assembled. For the first time in Micronesia the letter from Kamehameha was read and interpreted. The missionary hymn was also sung, and, whatever it meant to heathen who listened, it was full of significance to missionaries who had come so far and hoped so much. Mrs. Gulick speaks for them all: —

"Our feelings none can imagine but those who have realized a similar scene. Perfect silence prevailed, and our hearts rose in joyful hope at least. 'Salvation! O salvation!'"

Still, neither king nor chiefs committed themselves to a permanent welcome of the missionary. The hope of a better religion meant little to them. Their own, a vague sense of a Supreme Being, and a mild type of ancestral worship, satisfied them. "Spirit-stones" stood in many places, and to these monthly offerings were made. A god offended was placated by a feast. Superstition was their master, though they boasted neither idol, priest, nor temple.

Of this new thing and this new people they were suspicious. They feared interference with their customs, especially with their plan for plurality of wives. In any case the missionaries would visit other islands before deciding where to locate.

And from the midst of human beings who swam like fish about her the Caroline sailed away from the quiet lagoon, out again into the Pacific.

Butaritari was but one of sixteen coral islands that formed the Kingsmill or Gilbert Archipelago, a typical coral group, more compact than any other in Micronesia; a group of wreaths that rested lightly on the ocean, or better, a group of buried islands made immortal by the wreaths that grace their resting place. At least this they are to those who hold that each once surrounded an island now buried, and that, while the central island sank, the tireless coral insect kept pace with it in the upbuilding of a wall about it, until, passing through all the stages from fringing to encircling reef, it stands at last complete, an island that man may live upon, an atoll, the lonely representative of the island it formerly guarded.

These atolls are indeed picturesque. A narrow strip of land, half a mile wide, enclosing quiet water; white sands that border on the lagoon within, and sand as white that faces all the Pacific outside. Between the two are trees that form the wreath, cocoanuts always facing the lagoon, bending slightly toward it as if in greeting, and pandanus on the ocean side. One grows best when shielded, the other when resisting the tempest.

Under these cocoanut trees that tower thirty, forty, fifty feet above the coral, and under these spreading pandanus trees, forty thousand people lived upon the Gilbert Islands. From birth to death their only food was fish and cocoanut and pandanus; this was literally all they had to eat. Their drink was water, slightly brackish, and fermented cocoanut sap that intoxicated them.

Still further impoverishing them were storms that sometimes destroyed their fruit trees.

Of necessity political economists on the Gilbert Islands were Malthusian in their doctrines. Indeed, the relation of population to food supply was here an immediate and practical question. They solved it by systematic infanticide. No mother was allowed more than two or three living children. And war and pestilence were welcomed as the hope of the race.

Physically contrasted to low coral reefs and their depressing limitations was Kusaie, of the Caroline group. This was approached on the twenty-first of August. Not an atoll this time, but an island that as bravely held its head among the clouds as any hopeful visionary. From the deck of the Caroline they saw it twenty miles away. And, drawing nearer, every mile more clearly proved it a vision rising out of fairyland, nay, fairyland itself.

They anchored in what seemed a landlocked harbor. High hills wrapped in green from base to summit were its ancient sentinels; and spread out beneath waters clear as crystal were gardens and forests of shaded seaweed and coral. Under these forests was the beautiful sand, while among them and over them were the inhabitants of the place. Here were shells of every hue and shape that slowly moved about. Here, too, were crabs that scuttled around in funny sidewise fashion; starfish as blue as the skies above them, and merry little fish that played in groups and watched the canoe that glided above them, and darted away in wildest glee among the coral branches. Here and there a youthful shark lazily cut the air with its dorsal fin; and lying on the sandy bed a giant sting ray with hideous face and unwinking eye gazed silently upward at the sun.

As if all this were not beauty enough for voyagers in a Kusaiean canoe, for half a mile there was the added witchery of moving under the shadow of wide-reaching mangrove trees, trees that tropic luxury in growing seemed to have crowded from the land out into the mouths of the streams and on to the rich basaltic mud of the coral flats. Almost the only tree that grows in salt water, here it thrived luxuriantly; at high tide a noble forest walking out to sea; at low tide a discouraged forest patiently wading back on stilts through the mud. For the strong, long, and twisted roots were dismally exposed when high tide left them.

Birds singing in branches above them; fish sporting in water below them; the flecking of sunshine and shadow around them; surely nature was very kind and beautiful on Kusaie. No wonder Dr. Gulick felt it, and, carried away by the enchantment, copied into his journal : —

> There's beauty in the deep;
>   The wave is bluer than the sky;
>   And though the light shines bright on high,
> More softly do the sea gems glow
> That sparkle in the depths below.
>
> The rainbow tints are only made
> When on the waters they are laid,
>   And sun and moon most sweetly shine
>   Upon the ocean's level brine.
> There's beauty in the deep.

Two islands form the empire of Kusaie. In 1852 the population of the whole was fifteen hundred. Their king was known as good King George, and his subjects suggested the Chinese in personal appearance. They were a delicate, slender people of light copper color and small features. Their black eyes were sunken and slightly oblique in their setting, while their hair was long and fine and black, and neatly tied upon itself at the side or back of the head. They wore no garment for warmth in Micronesia, simply a braided mat about the waist. When the Kusaiean dude sighed for style a flannel shirt was added. For style, too, many pretty ears were bored; and by constant stretching these lobes were so drawn out like rubber that in time they were useful no less than ornamental. In these extended ears flowers were carried instead of earrings. In them, too, did the aspirant after imported fashions sometimes carry his shirt when he crossed a stream or swam to meet a whaler. Here, too, the pipe was often stored away — pipe in one ear, shirt in the other; all that civilization had brought to them packed thus conveniently in their Micronesian saratogas.

A pleasant-mannered people this was who came to meet the Caroline. Many of them talked broken English, as learned from whalers. The combination of heathen costume with English words and manners was sometimes unique; notably so when the king's son took tea with the missionaries. An evident heathen, with only his shirt as a visible mark of civilization, yet in calm self-possession he sat in a chair drawn up to a table neatly spread, and with knife, fork, and spoon ate the food of Western lands. With a napkin he touched his lips. And in quiet dignity he talked the language of the antipodes and answered questions which these people from the antipodes asked him.

"What do you think of missionaries?" they ventured.

There was no hesitation in the answer, shrewdly

noncommittal: "Bad captains tell me missionaries bad; good captains tell me missionaries good."

When asked whether or not he would like to go to America, he sat silent for a moment, then said abruptly: "What use me go America? Me got no money."

The golden goddess of America so large that even heathen Micronesia saw it!

By special appointment missionaries from America and Hawaii soon called on good King George of Kusaie. Royalty met them graciously. It proved a higher type than was found on Butaritari. Indeed, royalty on Kusaie was the highest type in Micronesia. The palace itself proved this, and the king was its explanation. With Eastern courtesy he met his visitors at the doorway; and with the cordial grace of sixty years and the self-possession which comes from assured superiority he welcomed them each with a smile, a handshake, and a sincere "Good-morning."

Then he led them into his palace. This was a large straw-thatched building with posts and reeds firmly tied together for walls. A square fireplace was in the center; a bed raised a foot from the ground in one corner; reed matting on the floor; and over all a pervading air of neatness and order. In addition visitors soon realized that there was much here in the line of imported luxury, for the seats they occupied were foreign chests, while conspicuously placed about the room — the palace — were guns, saws, a lantern, a few water-colored prints, and a lamp. "Exhibiting," as Dr. Gulick says, "King George's wealth as Solomon might have exhibited his peacocks and monkeys from Tarshish."

Seated on the floor, affectionately playing with her grandchild, was the queen. Diminutive, old, and wrinkled, she was nevertheless most youthfully clad in a short-sleeved, low-necked, calico gown that came to her knees.

To the king and queen presents were given: a Hawaiian Bible and hymn book, Cheever's Island World with its illustrations, two red flannel shirts, a red blanket, red petticoat, turkey-red calico as a gown for the queen, and scissors to be gracefully suspended from her royal neck by the red ribbon which accompanied them.

The interview was pleasant. Its result: permission that a missionary and his wife should live on Kusaie; only one white couple at first; and the explanation for this restriction was in the terse remark of the king: "Like one white man come; not many. If many come, rum come, fight come."

His sentiments on the temperance question were indeed manifest everywhere. Total prohibition was the law of the land; a law so strenuously enforced that he allowed no cocoanut tree to be tapped on Kusaie. To tap the tree secured a pleasant drink. Once fermented, this would intoxicate. People intoxicated were noisy and disagreeable; therefore the prohibition. Or, in the more forceful words of King George himself: "Plenty white men speak me very good; tap cocoanut tree get toddy. Me say no, no good. Plenty men get drunk on shore; too much row; me like all quiet; no tap cocoanut tree on Kusaie."

And that was the end of it. Kusaicans did not get drunk. An autocrat in heathen Micronesia was able to enforce temperance legislation. Polygamy was also prohibited; and stealing met its swift retribution. A thief was whipped while the missionaries were there — evidently the usual treatment, for speaking in idiomatic English, the king, turning to them, said: "That is the way we treat men here who steal."

In truth, good King George was a remarkable man. Chosen by acclamation of the people to succeed a tyrant he had helped depose, he gave up his preference for fishing and ruled over the Kusaicans as a wise and righteous father. And they, in turn, to show their love and respect for him, spoke in lowered tones when he was near; they even whispered, silenced the dogs, and approached him on their hands and knees.

Done voluntarily at first, this had now become so much the custom of the land that even his son was under its requirement.

Witness the inherent nobility of this man. Forgetting that he is only a semi-clad heathen, and that these men before him are representatives of a mighty civilization and of a religion which they have come to teach him; remembering only that he is a man, and that they too are but men who seem sincere and kind and helpful, when they asked him what his message was to the king of Hawaii, he quietly answered in flawless English: "Tell him that I will be a father to Mr. and Mrs. Snow."

And this till the end he always was.

Thus does it happen that, in the Central Pacific, on an island remote since the beginning from civilization and Christianity; on an island touched only by the blight which whalers often carry with them from Christian lands, good King George towers in Micronesian history as Abraham among the nations. For accepting truth all that such a man needed was to hear it. And this was soon possible. He gave land for a mission home and promised to help in its building when Mr. and Mrs. Snow should return. And when, as they left Kusaie, he shook hands again and said "Good-by," it was as if a patriarch had blessed them.

No need to speak of encouragement and thanksgiving and light hearts that sailed still farther westward in the Caroline. Verily, for nine bright days hope moved among the stars, for who could tell but larger welcome yet would meet them on Ponape?

CHAPTER XII.

REACHING PONAPE.

AS the Caroline drew near to Ponape, there first appeared the wide-encircling barrier reef, an outline whitened for eighty miles by breakers that dashed against it, and studded already with islets formed upon it; a coral reef that met, on one side, the fury of every storm that swept the Pacific, and on the other faced eternal peace.

Within the reef, an emerald gem in a white coral setting, was Ponape itself, the largest of forty-eight islands that formed the Caroline group, and the one by which all Micronesia had been judged. Pictured simply, Ponape is an island sixty miles in circumference, with an average height of twenty-five hundred feet. At that time it had ten thousand inhabitants. Yet, as the Caroline approached, not a house was seen through draping vines and shining moss and splendid trees that mantled it from summit to seashore.

Missionaries and crew were alike excited; and watching the scene with them, we too "advance toward the tree-girt shore. The breeze seems by a rebound from the hills to subside with the sea. We are evidently approaching one of nature's sanctuaries. We glide more and more gently. The sailor at his post eyes the paradise with the knowing look of one who has seen the world and will be surprised at nothing, while his whole soul is evidently stirred as he responds to the vigorously uttered command from the quarter-deck by a more than prompt 'Ay, ay sir,' and a dashing obedience that spins the vessel from side to side."

Soon, from the islets of the reef, from sandy beach and quiet lagoon, graceful canoes glide out to meet the Caroline; some speed to the rhythmic movement of paddles; some have white triangular sails that gleam like silver in the sunlight — thirty canoes in all. And to the Caroline, across the hush of expectation, there rolls " a swelling wave of subdued chattering." Does it signify war or peace? In each canoe five natives; twelve white faces among them; a company that proves homes somewhere and humanity to fill them. There is tense life in the graceful form that stands erect, fearless and proud, in the quivering prow of his slight canoe. Surely a fine type of island manhood this: eyes keen and black that pierce the waters ahead; skin copper-colored, neatly tattooed, polished with cocoanut oil till it shines like a mirror; hair short, black, and glossy, adorned with a head-dress of beads; and for costume a skirt of young cocoanut leaves, a necklace of shells and beads, and cardrops gorgeous with red flannel and beads.

Here too is island grace, for the belle herself has come to meet the foreigner. Hands and feet are saffron-stained for beauty. Turkey-red cloth is wrapped about her limbs, and a bright handkerchief partially covers chest and shoulders. With a gigantic taro leaf she shields herself from tropic sunshine, and in easy nonchalance she watches the people about her.

Pilots and chiefs and shining natives soon crowded the decks of the Caroline; and it would be difficult to picture the excitement of the days that followed. Instead of war it was reiterated welcome. This, not because on Ponape they hungered for righteousness, but because they certainly did hunger for the trade which white men had always brought them; for riches in guns, powder, and tobacco which came from that mysterious land which stretched out beyond the horizon somewhere.

But most surprising was the welcome that the missionaries received from " a tall, slim, bronzed man," who came as a pilot to meet them. With the ease of a Frenchman he touched the tortoise-shell front to his close-fitting cap, and with earnest sincerity told them how he had prayed for missionaries, and how he thanked God that at last they had come!

Twenty years of sinning on Ponape, followed by

illness and fear and repentance and prayer, explained that welcome from Mr. Corgat. Prayers in Micronesia drawing them; prayers in America and Hawaii sending them, and Mr. Corgat waiting for them there on Ponape with his childlike faith and his simple welcome!

"As the tide was low," writes Dr. Gulick, "we immediately commenced that course of wading and dragging and sweltering so long our privilege on this heathen island; only that, fortunately, our first experiences were enlivened by the romance of novelty, and were relieved from real labor by efficient natives. We had not yet acquired that carelessness regarding the immersion of shoes in salt water which soon grew upon us, and were content to be handled like babes, to be carried on in advance of the canoes, and to be left perched on toppling stones while the natives returned to drag the canoes toward us." All this was necessary because "the waters enclosed within the barrier reef were our only roads," as Dr. Gulick says, "and our passages, even for short distances, are very much regulated by the tides, the observance of which is, therefore, more important to us than that of our clocks."

Ponape was reached on the sixth of September. On the 29th the Caroline sailed away. Dr. and Mrs. Gulick, Mr. and Mrs. Sturges, and Mr. and Mrs. Kaaikaula were left there, while Mr. and Mrs. Snow with Mr. and Mrs. Opunui were taken back to Kusaie. The Caroline then moved out again into the world, and Christian history in Micronesia opened its first chapter. Perhaps it was as well that its heroes, ready for self-denial, could not know what the measure of it was to be.

CHAPTER XIII.

SMALL BEGINNINGS.

THE story of those years in Micronesia is very simply told by those who lived it. It showed a life of mingled threads; study of the language, preaching and teaching, medical work, physical discomfort, mental hunger, the annual mail, disappointment, heartache, encouragement, and hope. These were the various threads that formed the warp and woof of daily living. But first of all came acquaintance with the people.

"Let the philanthropist and friend of missions but vividly realize the heathen's infancy," writes Dr. Gulick, "and his wonder will cease that generations must lapse before a race can be civilized.

"As in the hotbeds of American democracy, that latest development of modern civilization, there are no children, only infants and men, so on Ponape. The Ponapean passes from infantile dirt to the niceties of a dandy. His head is as carefully oiled as that of anyone else. He has as much to say as anyone. He takes as important part in providing for the family as any other individual. Who may then obstruct his personal liberty? Not but that the father commands and the youth obeys, but the obedience is as optional with the youth as the command with the father.

"No Solomon has taught, on Ponape, the blessings of the rod, and woe to the parent who should insanely attempt its application! Indeed, no Ponapean has the remotest conception of punishment from other impulse than that of anger. No word in the language conveys the idea of deliberate, just retribution for misdeeds."

Further, of their moral character he says: —

"How difficult to sustain hope in one's heart when planning for the elevation of a people whose contact with the representatives of civilization serves, with but few exceptions, to render their diseases more deadly, their vices more vicious!"

When foreign missionaries reached Ponape, eighty foreigners were leading godless lives there, and Dr. Gulick exclaimed: —

"How numerously does Satan commission his non-salaried missionaries!"

Still the new life had now begun among the Ponapeans and the record of it. Over and over again we read the words "Rono Kiti" and "Matalanim" until we learn to know that these are the two most important of the five tribes of Ponape; that each gives its name to a harbor; that they are separated from each other by twenty-five miles of water — this their only line of communication; that they are rival tribes frequently at war, and that Mr. and Mrs. Sturges with Mr. and Mrs. Kaaikaula live at Rono Kiti, while Dr. and Mrs. Gulick are alone at Matalanim.

Thus separated, even missionaries on the same island could not often see each other. Indeed, Mrs. Gulick and Mrs. Sturges seldom met more than once or twice a year. Of necessity also, missionary work, though similar in character, was to a large extent carried on separately in the Matalanim and Rono Kiti tribes.

The year 1853 found their Micronesian life fairly begun. Dr. Gulick had built for himself a home on beautiful Shalong Point on the shores of Matalanim harbor. A "woe-begone Englishman" helped him build it. Four weeks from the day the foundations were laid the young couple entered their own first home and began housekeeping in Micronesia.

Curiosity speculates as to what sort of house that was at Shalong, erected in four weeks and costing one hundred and seventy dollars. It is easy to answer the query, for we are told somewhat about it: —

"The floor of our house consisted of thick poles hewn on the upper surface; the sides and partitions were of reed wickerwork through which tropical breezes sometimes blew quite too freely; the roof and broad veranda were thatched with sago leaves." This was the happy home of scorpions, lizards, and centipedes, "a roofing very satisfactory, however," as Dr. Gulick used to say, " so long as the leaves lay down the right way. But when the wind blew them up, the water poured the wrong way; and many times did I have to mount the roof in the rain to keep dry!"

This one-story home measured twenty feet by thirty. A hall through its center was reception and dining room combined, and schoolroom too for a season. On either side the hall were the four rooms — library, bedroom, spare room, and pantry. The kitchen stood apart from the house, a room by itself.

In the library, arranged on homemade, unpainted shelves, were treasures more precious than gold to Dr. Gulick — his books; four hundred volumes safely lodged at last in his own home. From the window of this library, eyes soon learned to turn instinctively beyond the green edging of the Pacific, beyond the whitened barrier reef, across old ocean that stretched away illimitably, eyes that watched eagerly through weeks and through months for some message from the world that was beyond it all.

In this work of building which they had undertaken, Dr. Gulick and Mr. Sturges were from the outset met by the question as to how far they were justified in using tobacco as a medium of exchange with the people. With it all the wealth of Ponape might be purchased, food and labor, friends even and pupils. Without it there was often poverty and actual suffering.

Both in the Hawaiian Islands and in the American Board rooms in Boston there was strenuous opposition to its use in any possible form. To use it as a medium of exchange was to countenance its use as a narcotic: thus to use it was a sin; all, therefore, who had any dealings with it were sinners; so they seemed to reason.

But when, in dire extremity, neither Mr. Sturges nor Dr. Gulick could secure help in building their homes without it they yielded to the inevitable, bought some from a whaler and used it "with consciences void of offense," as Dr. Gulick wrote, "for the pathway seemed and still seems very clear."

"You are aware," he further says, "that the use, the morality and the religion of the use, of tobacco is one that has much exercised the Hawaiian Islands Mission, and that the missionaries there are, in the main, on the extreme of orthodoxy. Whether in Micronesia we shall, whether we can, maintain the same rigidity is now the question."

Then with a smile through the writing, yet with serious intent, Dr. Gulick tells the officers of the American Board that "should Micronesia take the extreme position and should natives there learn the English language, the publications of the American Board of Commissioners for Foreign Missions must pass through inquisitorial censorship before they can be placed in the hands of our disciples; and that too," he adds, "from their lurking heresy on this doctrine." To illustrate he refers them to the April number of The Dayspring for 1852; and with a twinkle in eyes that follow his pen he tells them that it "represents a missionary who is most commendatorily noticed as one who has borne hardship for Christ," the Rev. Hugo Hahn, who, "comfortably mounted on an ox, musket in hand, has a countenance that wears the semblance of holy calmness and true Germanic happiness. But whether this comes from an ignorant or indurated conscience, it is, alas, too painfully palpable that he is already a guilt-condemned TOBACCO SMOKER!! And I am at this moment obliged to hide it away lest it meet the eyes of our bright-sighted Litobo, and lest she should ask, 'Is that a missionary?'"

Then very seriously he begs not to be misunderstood and assures the Board that he will ever "oppose the extravagant and general use of tobacco on physiological and economic premises, but not, at present at least, on moral and religious grounds further than as physiology and economics touch on morality."

However, in deference to conservative home opinion, tobacco was never used on Ponape except in cases of extreme emergency — even then sparingly. Missionaries often endured the suffering of physical privation rather than bring offense to brethren in home lands who could not or would not understand the situation on Ponape. Of necessity, however, tobacco had helped build homes for the missionaries.

With prompt civility, neighbors filled with curiosity came from far and near to call upon the strangers. Interesting types the callers were sometimes. Once it was a priest who " strutted up to our door dressed in a flaming red flannel shirt and a cocoanut leaf skirt, with an umbrella over his head "— attire as religiously inspiring, perhaps, in Micronesia as enlarged borders and widened phylacteries in Jerusalem. At another time there came what Dr. Gulick describes as " an old mummy of a priest with a leathern-skinned face, who could pull the corners of his mouth almost to his eyes and who could wink so forcibly as to almost obliterate the space between the hairs of his head and his eyebrows."

Even royalty visited them sometimes, for there were two marvels now at Shalong that charmed alike the earthly and the heavenly minded. Who, indeed, could resist the small melodeon that stood in the hallway and the fair-haired woman who played upon it? Yet there was comedy of sensation one day when the Matalanim king himself brought a royal guest to hear the music.

To relieve his tired wife, Dr. Gulick made no apology but courageously took her place at the melodeon, "the suspicion not crossing my mind," as he says, "but that my performance would be as highly appreciated as my wife's, albeit I have no knowledge of either the science or the practice of music. I sat down to the instrument, put my feet in proper position on the pedals, placed my fingers on the keys and moved them up and down on the counter, swaying my body the while as musicians do, and producing sounds such as I supposed were without doubt softening the savage heart as music is said always to do. Imagine then my surprise on hearing my greasy king apologizing to the still more untutored stranger chief, saying, 'The foreign man knows nothing about it; it is the woman.'"

That was the end of Dr. Gulick's musical recitals. Indeed, by natural division of labor Mrs. Gulick was organist, housekeeper, and school-teacher, while Dr. Gulick was physician, carpenter, student, and preacher.

Naturally enough, each department was full of interest and also of trial. School work meant native curiosity at first, a fear of foreign witchery in learning to read, heroism in those who first dared attempt it, and a frightened king who turned almost pale when a small boy wrote his name upon a slate, and later read it to him.

Then, however, came the era of growing courage that ended in enthusiasm. Yet fear and enthusiasm were alike most natural; for Micronesian eyes had never yet seen Micronesian words in writing. The wildest Ponapean imagination had never dreamed it. As a result, teachers and pupils too faced the difficulties of an unwritten language and the lack of a printing press. Missionaries, however, rapidly caught simple words and phrases. These were written down. Gradually a primer grew, one leaf at a time. Of this primer hand-written copies were made. These were lent to aspiring students, and these students taught each other.

Ambition spread her wings. One boy had read to the bottom of the page; another had turned the leaf. Men and women joined the number. No outward sign yet proved the budding erudition. Cocoanut oil, tattooing, brown skins were all as before; but earnestly gathered in hall and veranda were men, women, and children, bending over the whole Micronesian literature, a hand-written primer, and learning to read it. It must have been a curious sight.

They came for instruction at any time from sunrise to sunset. And why not? What was time on Ponape? No sewing to be done; no professional duties; no farming; seldom any cooking; nothing but existence and acceptance of the goods that sunshine and kind fortune brought them. So now, at Shalong they were reading.

In due time there came the examination and the

exhibition. Then, to emphasize the outward effect that inward learning gives, Mrs. Gulick utilized the only material she had and the school shone forth resplendent, six girls in calico dresses that were blue, and four boys in calico sacks that were green. The æsthetic sense of Ponape was touched, and immediately school attendance was increased.

But this is anticipating. The exhibition was not till 1854, after native women had learned to sew.

Before this, while still the people came to study at irregular times, Mrs. Gulick was making the serious experiment of keeping house on Ponape. In truth it was a grave undertaking, this housekeeping in a land where neither cook nor maid had ever used knife, or fork, or spoon, or plate, or broom; among a people who, never having used vessels of metal or pottery, did not know that water boiled; who shrewdly considered chairs and tables and beds as the needless luxuries of a weakened humanity. Yet, such as they were, Mrs. Gulick had at first no difficulty in securing servants. These were always young boys ready to earn a shirt or a hatchet, the reward of service. What profit to them was money? For, as they said: "We can neither eat it nor wear it."

Unfortunately, however, even shirts had their drawbacks. They induced worldly thoughts, demoralized these Micronesian youths, made them haughty and proud, raised them "above their station." And this, though in the beginning it was difficult to enforce the regulation that no boy should do household duties without the adornment of a shirt. Unaccustomed sun-browned bodies had instinctively rebelled against these fetters of civilization. Yet in time they yielded so far as to inspire the following brief serio-comic history of civilization: —

"Our native boy did very well till I gave him a shirt. He then became of more consequence in his own eyes, and avoided all outdoor work. About two weeks since I gave Olel and Laiten each a pair of trowsers. This seemed to throw them very nearly off their balance. They began to be impudent. Yesterday Laiten sold both his shirt and trowsers for a bottle of grog; and now he is striding about as destitute as ever. But there is one good thing about it: he is not so impudent without his trowsers."

Verily, a life of mixed necessities this was on Ponape, where manners no less than morals and education waited to be molded by the missionary. In addition Dr. Gulick was, at different times, many other things: cook, shoemaker, carpenter, blacksmith, dressmaker, no less than spiritual guide and inspiration of the nation; and at Shalong each vocation seems to have had its period.

In 1855 Dr. Gulick was preëminently a carpenter.

During this year there sprang up near his home a straw-thatched group of buildings, as potent for good, as beautiful perhaps in angels' eyes as that other wonderful group at Pisa. Instead of cathedral, baptistry, and campanile, here were chapel, schoolhouse, and hospital. Instead of white marble and sculptured columns and hallowed earth from Palestine, here were rough-hewn logs, and reeds and straw. Instead of vast expense and skilled architects, here the material was had for its cutting, and the bishop himself did most of the work.

We follow this building from day to day and realize the physical strain it was to one who had never really toiled with his hands before: —

"Spent the whole day in work; erected the frame of my so-called hospital."

"Worked all the afternoon up to my knees in water getting out timber for building."

"I pray for grace to enable me to make even my physical labors tend to missionary usefulness."

"Worked hewing out logs for washstand and pulpit stand. Set up new bedstead in our room. How I grudge the time!"

Through this year there were natives to be hired sometimes and trade that secured them. Tobacco would always have done it; but by the last of 1854 novelty and hatchets and knives and beads and shirts all failed together. Mrs. Gulick was ill for months, and a new dilemma confronted the missionary enthusiasm of Dr. Gulick. Could it be that this was the work to which he had been called? But there was no alternative. From the carpenter's bench he moved to the kitchen, and with serious face and zeal that did not flinch the student who had grown up in the library with his pen worked as untiringly now with stove and broom and soapsuds as ever he had worked with Hebrew, Greek, and Latin.

After it was all over, from a distance far enough to soften hard outlines and lend proverbial enchantment to the view, the experience was interesting. At the time, however, it was hard. The journal does not complain; it simply states facts in a series of laconic items. For successive months these facts include very stern realities of housework, and there is the monotony of sameness about them: —

"Attended to meals, to washing clothes, and to getting firewood."

"So fatigued with household work and with mending my back veranda that I retire early."

"Last night mended my own and Louisa's shoes. The next time I shall succeed more like a workman."

"I am doing very little direct missionary work. Our hearts ache; but what can we do? Wife is sick. Nearly all the household and outdoor work falls on myself alone, washing and everything. We have had a nurse for a short period, otherwise we have had no help for about four months."

"Washed clothes, got breakfast, and while doing it read some." As sedately recorded as if reading and cooking were a normal combination! Indeed, there is no abatement yet to the thirsty desire for thoughts and books which have ever characterized Dr. Gulick.

"Wife sick. Went to Takain. Bought a canoe. Got dinner. Read Gibbon. Meditated on sermon for to-morrow."

"Rose before daylight, which is my habit, for the purpose of securing a little time for my Greek Testament and private preparation for the day."

"Not felt well. Planted bananas. Made bread and pudding. Read Father Bipa's Residence in China. Wife sick."

"Would that tears of sorrow could avail against these difficulties! Prayerful tears may; we therefore pray much. The hardest labors would be easier than this forced, struggling, inglorious quiescence."

"Hope ever! Good shall yet come out of this apparently fruitless life."

Then again, later:—

"I do seem to need a servant. My salary will hardly pay for keeping a foreigner, yet I seem to myself hardly the person for a cook. Mr. Sturges has been in the same difficulty for over a year. He is not yet delivered. Am I to remain in the same for as long a time? I pray for grace."

Mrs. Gulick, from her sick bed, wrote to her mother: —

"I am so weak and Halsey is all in all; but it does not seem right for such a man to spend months in domestic service. Yet think not we are disheartened. No, no; we are often merry and almost forget our troubles. We love to praise our heavenly Father for the innumerable blessings that still abound to us."

Doubtless there were blessings, yet to us, at this distance, verily life's trials overshadowed them. One trial that towered high sometimes was the difficulty they had in securing food. In 1853 they already suffered physically from lack of fresh meat. All the meat they had was salted. In 1854 when trade failed and annual supplies had not yet come, they sometimes went to bed hungry. For without the equivalent for money, food was no more easily bought in Micronesia than in New York. Indeed the missionary in Micronesia was under peculiar disadvantage. He kept neither firearms nor powder, nor liquor nor tobacco. These were gold on Ponape always at par. The more fluctuating currency was represented by beads, knives, hatchets, and red flannel. When these were gone the wolf boldly looked in at the doorway; at times he even walked into the house.

"During these seasons of enforced scarcity," writes Dr. Gulick, "tropical fruit ripening over our heads without our being able to buy them, we fell back on our foreign supplies, consisting mainly of salted meats and flour. But these were often poor or quite uneatable from the dampness of the torrid zone. The flour in the barrels was often so caked by moisture that we had to cut it out with hatchets, and worms an inch long often developed in it numerously." Your pardon, gentle reader, but so it is written. And this was the flour they were trying to eat! "So long as we retained our health we got along very well, but when health and appetite both failed we were at a disadvantage."

"During shipping season, which is from October to May, it is difficult for us to purchase a breadfruit or bunch of bananas, or to hire a native for any purpose."

This is explained by the fact that the ships bought all that the natives cared to sell, and paid for what they bought in tobacco and powder. At such times Dr. Gulick shot wild pigeons. But his gun failed him and there was nothing for it but to endure; and then we trace the touching entries:—

"We are becoming quite needy. Will not the Lord soon provide and soon relieve us?"

"Received the present of a leg of pork from our chief. It is the first piece of fresh meat we have tasted in more than three months."

"We shall soon suffer if our supplies do not come."

Then Mrs. Gulick itemizes: —

"We are quite short of food now; indeed, never so short before and unable to buy. We have some most miserable salt beef, not a quarter of a barrel of flour, some tapioca, about one pound of butter, molasses and sugar, tea and coffee. This with arrowroot and a little preserved ginger constitutes all our foreign food. We are living from hand to mouth almost, but trust in our Father's care."

"Halsey brought from Rono Kiti about a pint of fresh milk, which was the first I had seen since we left the Hawaiian Islands nearly three years ago."

Later she adds: "We have succeeded in purchasing from a captain two hundred pounds of flour and two hundred pounds of hard bread, which will keep us all from being hungry." Or, as Dr. Gulick expresses it, "This will keep us from starvation." So once more ravens fed the prophet!

And this was Micronesia! this the altar of his sacrifice; this the high point of all his preparation! Did there come a sense of sweeping disappointment as of sacrifice larger than was needed? We do not know.

From first to last no whisper of disappointment is recorded, but the whole journal with its minutiæ, its pathos, its self-unconsciousness, reads like a romance to hearts that realize what isolation and privation sometimes meant in Micronesia.

CHAPTER XIV.

ISOLATION AND MENTAL ACTIVITY.

To missionaries prepared to meet it, the prospect of isolation had not seemed overwhelming when the Caroline left, to come again once a year. Yet unconsciously they centered all their hope of physical and mental life upon her regular visits, and with no thought of disappointment they waited for her coming.

She returned to them once, and then, after many months, a whaler brought letters which told them that, because it cost so much to send her every year, the Caroline had been sold, and that in future both mail and supplies would be sent to Micronesia by whalers as the opportunity offered itself in Honolulu. This was so unexpected that missionary heroism was staggered for a moment; and though in reply Dr. Gulick assured the Hawaiian Missionary Society that, in view of its lack of funds, he had "not the least doubt but that its action was in every respect for the best," still his pain could not be concealed.

"Our hearts received a stunning blow," he writes, "when we heard that the only cord of connection between ourselves and the Christian world was by their act dissevered, and that, so far as the slightest extra provision was made, we were left to sink or swim, as God might please. Our hearts almost rebelled."

This irregularity of communication continued until 1857, when children's pennies sent the Morning Star to Micronesia. Of whalers who, in the meantime, visited them, some only had touched at Honolulu; and among these but few secured and brought the mail to Micronesia.

The shipping season continued from October to May. Naturally, therefore, with the first of October missionaries on Ponape began to look daily, almost hourly, for their annual mail. Often it was late in coming. At such times slow days rolled on into the weeks. Six months passed without a letter from the world; ten months even; twelve months, and still no letter. Ship after ship appeared on the horizon, crossed the shining, wide ocean, and reached harbor at last. But to the eager inquiry for mail and supplies there came, over and over again, the same answer: "We have nothing for you."

As months passed, the earnest desire of these missionaries became an almost hopeless cry for help. The luxuries of life were gone; its bare necessities very low; and who can measure their famishing mental hunger? To have body and mind both starve on Ponape were tragic indeed, yet both were threatened sometimes.

Dr. and Mrs. Gulick do not speak very often of the pain this isolation brought them, but we easily trace it: —

"My heart would hardly be quieted at night as I felt that nine ships had disappointed us."

"We scan the horizon every morning with the deepest interest, and the shout of 'Chop! chop!' thrills through all our frame."

"Thirteen ships have anchored in the harbor of this island, yet only one brought us letters."

"There are times in our beloved Micronesia when we are put upon looking toward the unseen to keep our hearts from utter failure."

"It is hard to let go our last links to the outside world. But we may erelong learn to be content alone with the remembrance of our heavenly Father."

"Our hearts are sick, our souls faint, our eyes wearied in the watching."

Then, at last, beyond the canoes and the natives that frolicked in the water, beyond the fringing reef and the breakers, "eyes wearied in the watching" saw the outline of another sail. 'This time it was the ship they waited for; and when it came natives too rejoiced, for they too had hopes in the annual mail.

Perchance it would bring to them beads and fishhooks, red flannel and shirts!

After thirteen months of such waiting once, Dr. Gulick confessed to "an almost nervous fever that had preyed upon them." "Day by day," he says, "and many times a day, have our eyes involuntarily ranged the horizon. Minute darkened clouds, to our ready imagination, have assumed the appearance of Ascension Island bound vessels. The peculiar shouting of the natives when a ship was certainly in sight has thrilled us like shocks of electricity. As these ships have passed along our coast for one of the more southern harbors of the island, with what excited nerves have we attempted to perform our regular routine of missionary work, till in some way we have definitely learned, two or three days later, that there was no mail on board.

"Nor does our excitement abate with the actual arrival of the thirteen months' mail. On its first announcement, how the heart leaps! The canoe is hastily launched, the paddles splash the brine regularly, the sail almost spontaneously spreads itself; and so we speed along for perhaps twenty miles. The magic package of letters is at last secured. The fever is at its height. The crisis arrives. Envelope after envelope is rapidly torn, its contents barely skimmed. Thrills of joy and spasms of sorrow flash through us, till at last the overstrained nerves almost cease to react under either stimulation. The face is flushed; the mind confused; the heart surcharged. We return to our home to reread the budget more at leisure and talk it over and dream it over. A twelve months' mail is a blessed privilege, but a sad shock."

Letters which whalers carried to the world from Ponape were passed on by them to others, and usually reached America via China, the Okotsk Sea, and Honolulu; and because the tide of shipping was all in the same direction, even letters to the missionary neighbors on Kusaie followed the same circuitous route, reaching their destination at last from Hawaii.

Thus also were orders sent once a year for all the foreign goods that Micronesia needed — provisions for a year, material for building, tools, and trade, furniture and clothing. And those orders spent a year in going, the supplies a year in coming. They were used the third year.

It must have taken the keenness of a prophet's eye to anticipate wants in Micronesia two years before they were felt! Who could tell that a stove would so rust at Shalong that a new one would be needed in two years? Who could anticipate a fire that should consume Mr. Sturges' home in Rono Kiti and involve the cordial dividing of household goods at the other home in Shalong? Verily, though there be large measure of love, half a loaf divided leaves very little.

Ordering supplies was certainly important, but how measure the delight Dr. Gulick felt in sending his annual order for new books? Orders of varying size — seventy-five dollars one year, one hundred the next — large sums to spare from Micronesian salaries, but curtailment came on other things. Physical comforts they could forego; books they must have; therefore they sent for what they thought they needed. But disappointment came sometimes as a sequel; notably so after their first large order was sent.

For months, physical hunger, economy, and self-denial had been easier to bear because of what they thought this lack on one hand might mean of plenty on the other. Two years had passed; and now eyes strained every day over the horizon were looking for the annual mail and for the books. But what if breathless suspense were to go unrewarded this year? What if there were no mail? What if shipwreck had overtaken those books? So they questioned. And then the end came.

The mail arrived; but instead of books they received an almost incredible message. Agents acting for Dr. Gulick had refused to meet the bill for all the books he ordered. By some mistake they thought he had overdrawn his salary. Older heads felt wiser than the student there on Ponape, and using their discretion, they sent him what they thought he needed most.

No telegraph wires to summon his books; no ship to bring them; and two more years of waiting before they could reach him! Surely this was harder to meet bravely as a Christian than heathenism itself.

Though numbed by the pain of his disappointment, Dr. Gulick accepted the inevitable — what else was possible in Micronesia? But he took immediate action. He directed that an ox given him on Hawaii be sold, the proceeds to go for books. His only watch he sent to Honolulu, this also to be exchanged for books. The emergency was great.

"Books," he says, "are Louisa's and my life. They are more important to us than beef or pork, or even red flannel and red beads."

"We must have books if nothing else. To deprive us of them is cruelty."

As a brighter side to the picture, it is pleasant to know that Dr. Gulick's father, hearing that the books had not been sent, himself paid for them, and soon had opportunity to forward them to Ponape. It is also pleasant to know that friends everywhere increasingly realized that no libraries were found in Micronesia, and that four hundred dollars a year was small measure for the maintenance alike of body and mind. Remembering too that Dr. Gulick, buried in Micronesia, a missionary, was still human, still intellectual, still filled with a restless desire to keep pace with the thought of the world, they sent him books as gifts. In a single year thirty-five volumes came from his home church, the Broadway Tabernacle of New York city. Does the hungry man welcome food? Then we appreciate the welcome these books received.

"Thank you for the books," he says: "thank you over and over! My mind will be the livelier and my heart the holier, I hope."

Thus, even in Micronesia, the library grew. Four hundred volumes were soon increased to six hundred; and in 1859 twenty boxes carried Dr. Gulick's library of one thousand volumes from the narrow doorway of the cottage at Shalong.

Reading kept pace with the growing library. Pages might be filled, as they are in Dr. Gulick's journal, with simple mention of the books he read, and chapters might follow with his comments upon them. Little of all this can be introduced here, yet enough perhaps to show that these signs of mental life do not come as an echoing voice, as a plaintive wail from buried depths; but that they are the criticisms, the appreciation of an independent student.

"Am engaged in Biblical studies," he writes;

"Greek, Hebrew, and English. At intervals, also am pursuing my investigations regarding New England theology. Have been reading the younger Edwards and Mahan, of Oberlin. The latter has very little metaphysical talent, I fancy. He deals in assertions rather than reasonings on all the hinge questions."

"Have accomplished much in the study of Greek and of modern history during the past year, for which I am grateful."

Of Knox's "The Races," he says: "A somewhat original, but not a commendable writer. He belongs to the race of literary Ishmaelites. His science is assertion, his argument sarcasm, his wit a grin."

At greater length is the following, to his brother John, then at Williams College. It is significant of the freedom his mind held for itself, for it should be remembered that in 1856 theories of evolution were not so readily accepted as they are to-day.

After pages of close reasoning on the subject, he expresses little sympathy for "the unlearned and conservative Bible readers who are too ignorant or too perverse to read nature also"; for those who "with frivolous fear think the devil seizes all that science demonstrates to be under the operation of natural law."

As for the creation of life itself, he finds that "McCosh, like Miller, sets up a barrier very close to us and thinks that because science has not yet, in its very babyhood, learned how the properties of matter are so adjusted as to produce life, that therefore we must rise directly ' to the only known cause capable of producing it — the fiat of the Creator.'" Over this he grows impatient and exclaims: "Why thus put the extinguisher on our young science and force it to wish a divorce from religion?"

Thus from the smallness of Micronesia did Dr. Gulick reach out into the world of thought and lay hold upon it. The truth is he fought for mental life as a man in dire extremity fights for physical existence. In part, it was the same instinct of self-preservation that held him to it. Yet even here he saw danger lest studies "interfere with the highest efficiency of action."

"Action and study," he adds, "cannot be antagonistic. They are indispensable coadjutors; I cannot be a full-grown missionary without both." For this reason he combined the two. He wrote down his plans; he followed them faithfully; and when the month or year was ended he reviewed what he had done in the light of what he had intended to do.[1]

---

[1] The following is the outline planned for one month: —

I. *Study of Ponape language.* 1. By much conversation with the natives. 2. By filling out my vocabulary. 3. By preparing First Lessons. 4. By writing Scripture lessons.

II. *Teaching natives.* 1. Our domestics in English. 2. School in Ponape. 3. Religious conversations. 4. Sabbath exercises.

III. *Literary occupation.* 1. Missionary journals for Boston. 2. A

After such a plan sent once to a brother, — a plan to undertake through successive years, as recreation, the scientific study of geology, botany, conchology, ichthyology, etc., — he pauses suddenly, as if he realized that no one else could quite understand the situation, and a moment later adds a pathetic closing question, the key to his ceaseless activity: "You perhaps will think me planning much for the future, yet how else shall I keep myself from sinking under the stagnation of this Ponape life?"

To further help him were his magazines and papers,[1] and his comments on the news they brought him show how eagerly he followed the shifting circles of history. At best, however, he felt very far off from them, for all this reading and thinking and writing was slipped between months that were locked away in Micronesian solitude.

Like figures in a fairy tale who wake to action

few letters. 3. Medical thesis. 4. Morning and evening, Hebrew Bible. 5. New England Theology. 6. Ichthyology.

IV. *Physical labor.* 1. Preparation of canoe. 2. Building schoolhouse. 3. Finishing veranda. 4. Sides of my house.

[1] The order for one year was as follows: —
The Missionary Herald, New York Observer, The New York Independent, The New York Weekly Tribune, Littell's Living Age, The Christian Retrospect, The Scientific Annual, Stryker's American Register, The Princeton Review, The London Lancet, Braithwaite's Retrospect, The Medico-chirurgical Review, The Colonization Journal, The Peace Advocate, The American Messenger, The American Bible Society Record, The Baptist Missionary paper, The Church Missionary, The American and Foreign Christian Union, Stillman's American Journal of Science, The Smithsonian Bulletin. (This last was not sent to him.)

at stated intervals and then fall back to sleep again, so life seemed to pass on Ponape. Months of quiet found their climax in days of intensity, when friends and all the world drew near them at once; then the silence of utter separation shut them in again, the sleep that seemed eternal "in an eternal night."

Sometimes when he felt it most Dr. Gulick turned upon himself with stern questions. Sometimes there was the word of pity, of encouragement, and sometimes, though rarely dwelt upon, he paints a graphic picture of their quiet life: —

"For weeks and often for months together," he writes, "I neither see nor converse with a 'white face,' save my precious wife. I work in my garden, read and write in my pleasant library, paddle my canoe from place to place to tell of divine pardon, and occasionally paddle to Rono Kiti on some errand to my fellow missionary; and thus do my days float past, noiseless as unimpeded waves of air. It is with some difficulty we keep correct record of our days, there is so very little to distinguish one from another. We often temporarily lose or gain a day, and one of my fellow missionaries recently gained a whole week."

"I must bear up against the tendency of all things here to listless idleness."

"I must learn to be content with this sleepy Ponape life, for Providence has evidently led me into it."

"In this land of sleep no life could flow more quietly than mine. I can scarcely hear it ripple about me and am just conscious of motion."

"What an isolated being I am! How even the flow of my days! Perhaps it is as well. I shall be able to concentrate my mind the more."

From their loneliness they begged their praying friends to remember and to help them: —

"O my Christian brothers, I pray you not forget us!"

"Are we, indeed, remembered in the prayers of Christians? Assure us of it and we shall be the happier."

"We can scarcely realize we are remembered much when we hear from you only once a year. How we need your prayers!"

"My heart is sore all over."

"Do not forget us when you pray!"

"This is a desert land and our souls are hungry. Oh, my brothers, pray for us."

"Adieu; pray. HALSEY."

And this is no flight of imagination. No onlooker can breathe into that life in Micronesia more of pathos and of loneliness than was actually there, lived every day by men and women who were trying to lift an island world into Christian life.

CHAPTER XV.

FURTHER ACQUAINTANCE WITH PONAPE AND HER PEOPLE. — THE EPIDEMIC.

IN spite of this extreme isolation, enhanced, indeed, by it was the interest Dr. Gulick took in every question relating to Ponape itself and to the whole of Micronesia. He ordered and read all that he could find printed about the islands of the Pacific. He traced the probable course of migration as people in canoes were drifted from island to island by winds and by currents. He saw, too, the obscure line of change in language; the growing dissimilarity where islands were more and more widely separated from each other, and the increased poverty of language where these islands were so low by nature as to lack even a physical basis for mental outlook. He perceived also the evident original unity of most of these scattered island dialects.

So carefully did he study Micronesian geography that his descriptions of many of the islands are now incorporated in the sailing directions used by all mariners in that part of the Pacific. And where previously the Micronesian page in children's geographies had been a chaos of indefiniteness, obscurity, and blunder, light and order were introduced through his untiring efforts.

For his own satisfaction he wished to know the truth about the land of his adoption, and for the sake of the world, having arrived at conclusions satisfactory to himself, he published them.

The closest study of conditions was of necessity done on Ponape. Here he found and minutely reported the earliest native productions and the later increase of vegetable and animal wealth through foreign imports. Concerning animal life he shows that, before history had made any note of their arrival, there were on Ponape birds, rats, bats, lizards, centipedes, scorpions, ants, fleas, and flies; and that between 1832 and 1851, pigs, dogs, ducks, fowls, and cats were introduced.

Variety of stock increased more rapidly after missionaries came, and much of it was a source of astonishment to the simple-minded natives. Cats and dogs had seemed large, but how appalling was Mr. Sturges' cow! They first feared and then teased her; and when with her horns she tossed them into the bushes they were surprised and wanted to stone her.

Varieties of plant life also multiplied with the coming of the missionary. Every mail brought seeds from Hawaii and America; and these were planted with varying success. In a climate whose extremes of temperature were 72° and 89° a luxuriant tropical growth was to be expected. Yet even this did not insure success. Melon vines grew apace, "but," says Dr. Gulick, "rats eat our melons before they ripen. And to aggravate the matter, the natives eat cats!" Potato vines grew like splendid weeds, but after two years the potatoes themselves had degenerated to mere fibers. Why, indeed, should roots store nourishment for vines that never could need a reserve supply? Nature was thus an open book, teaching many practical lessons.

On Ponape and Kusaie alike there were massive architectural ruins that gave rapid wing to foreign imagination. On Ponape these ruins covered fifteen acres, and were so divided by canals as to seem a group of artificial islands. Each island was banked with stone to protect it from the wear of waves, and each was a regular parallelogram. Standing as part of these ruins were walls thirty feet high, six feet thick at the top, eighteen at the bottom, and terraced on the inside from base to summit. All were built of natural basaltic prisms, four, five, and six feet sided; sometimes ten feet long and two feet thick, and without mark of any edged tool upon them. Through these massive walls there were openings large enough to admit a creeping man, and within were vaults containing human bones. Here too a Spanish crucifix had been found, some beads also, and a silver triangle. But canals choked with tropic growth, broken walls and growing trees, luxuriant vines and fragrant blossoms concealing the ruins, told that ages had passed since they were built.

Romantic foreigners attributed the work to another race and to prehistoric times, to the day, perhaps, when Ponape and Kusaie were but parts of some vast continent now submerged; yet Kusaican tradition claimed the work for her own past, and tradition on Ponape faintly spoke of giants who had lived and wrought and died before the present race arrived.

But whether built by ancestors or by a previous race, Dr. Gulick caught the meaning of the inarticulate speech of these dumb witnesses. He felt for those who, having once lived, wished to be remembered; for men who " beneath cocoanut, breadfruit, orange, and banyan trees have left such worthy memorials of bygone ages." "No wonder," he adds, "that living descendants of such worthy ancestors walk proudly in the shadow of this greatness, a greatness more overpowering to them than to us, but respectable to any who consider with what meager appliances these Micronesian Sennacheribs and Pharaohs executed their despotic wills." " How interesting to find posthumous fame as potent on an island for ages separated from the mass of humanity as in any crowded center of empire!"

All that glory was past for Kusaie. But on Ponape, whatever the object in building had been, parts of these ruins were hallowed places still. In one, kings were buried; in another, spirits talked through priests to men; in still another, tradition placed a sacred pond, and within this pond a sacred eel that lived alone and hungered; and it was said that zealous priests, to feed it, walked silently backward to the spot, dropped the offering into the water, and breathlessly sped away. But with Saxon incredulity Dr. Gulick one day explored the region of this mystery and found neither water, pond, nor sacred eel.

Thus on Ponape did priests easily delude the people. But here, as elsewhere in Micronesia, idol worship was unknown. When spiritual longing touched the people they worshiped spirits and the shades of their ancestors. Not a graven image nor a temple made with hands had ever stood on Ponape. In their stead were hallowed spots where priests mumbled incantations and cheerful worshipers offered bloodless sacrifice. With food enough before them and feasting long enough continued, spirits were willing to speak through the priests who prophesied to believing people. Religion on Ponape was little else. Nothing evil was forbidden by it; yet back of all the prophesying and the sacrificing and the sinning was the voice of God within them — the unflinching moral nature that even here was recognized.

"Certainly," said the heathen when he was questioned; "we know it is wrong to steal and to kill and to lie. We feel it here," striking his breast. And Dr. Gulick testified: —

"These people have consciences, to which I appeal without hesitation on all the cardinal points of morality, and they respond correctly. It may, however, quite safely be said that they are destitute of pure moral principle. When truthful, honest, and virtuous, it is because present interest constrains; and generally even the strongest of present interests will not secure such high-principled action."

In pleasant human fashion the people loved their neighbors when they were lovable; and they were too good-natured to murder very often. But, so far as recorded, good King George of Kusaie is the one example in Micronesia of a man who before the advent of Christianity did right because it was right.

Their religion was heathenism in one of its most spiritual forms, and it was easy here to teach the spirituality of God — so easy that the natives at once found resemblance between their ideal and this God that missionaries told them was very real and ever present. As to a future life, however, Mrs. Gulick writes: "The chiefs are offended that the common people can go to the same heaven with themselves!" That seems to have been at first the extent of their religious thinking. Indeed, while health and prosperity continued there was no cry in Micronesia for a better faith; but when calamity threatened there was despair and awakened spiritual life. Such an awakening occurred for Ponape in 1854.

In April a foreign sailor, hopelessly ill with smallpox, had been placed on shore to die. His ship had sailed away and left him there. He died; and in spite of vigorous protest from the missionaries, natives gleefully appropriated the dead man's clothing and proudly arrayed themselves in it. With these contaminated garments the smallpox began its work. Even then, however, the missionaries hoped its victims might be few; but by the middle of May the last hope died. The disease was upon them with all its horror.

As if this were not enough, there was no vaccine matter on the island. Virus brought by Dr. Gulick had long ago lost its power, and other, ordered later, had not yet arrived.

In the line of immediate action Dr. Gulick saw that his only hope of helping the nation was through inoculation with the smallpox virus itself. On the eighteenth of May he therefore inoculated himself and five others. On the 29th he recognized in himself the smallpox fever, started homeward from Rono Kiti, was upset in his canoe, spent hours in cold water and wet clothing, and on arriving at Shalong retired alone to his small hospital — to die, if God willed, to recover and be the savior of the people, if he should spare.

For the safety of others he thus isolated himself; and while he watched his symptoms and waited to know the will of God, his wife, in their home, with aching heart and bitter tears, prayed to God for the life of her husband. And who may know what the agony of that praying was? On Ponape only God had power enough to help them, and he was invisible!

After two days of suspense the fever passed. Life and not death was before him; and now for six terrible months, through rain and through sunshine, Dr. Gulick and his fellow missionaries struggled with the pestilence. What a battle! Whole neighborhoods devoted themselves to the killing of pigs and dogs, to cooking, and to feasting — their reason the spreading epidemic. "Eat, therefore, and drink," they said, "for to-morrow we die." As a natural result, they often did die on the morrow.

In half-hearted faith priests tried to propitiate offended spirits; but there was universal belief that Ponapean spirits were powerless against the might of this foreign disease. Better, they suggested, to give

Dr. Gulick himself a great feast, that he might propitiate the stronger God of the white man; but even without a feast Dr. Gulick promised to pray for them. And how he prayed!

Yet still the epidemic spread. Even the white man's God seemed powerless against the might of his own disease; and at last priests on Ponape made formal demand, in the name of their gods and their afflicted people, for the life of this impotent messenger of a relentless foreign God. They demanded that he be shot. Most happily for themselves, however, a friendly king dared to defy spirits and priests alike. Stronger than Pilate under similar pressure, he did not surrender the young doctor to them.

Through May and June, as fast as the natives allowed it, they were inoculated. And to the missionaries it meant everything that was worth caring for on Ponape whether life or death should follow this inoculation.

Mercifully, the larger part lived. Confidence in missionary power and integrity revived. And by the middle of June stricken people by scores and by hundreds were turning to Dr. Gulick as their only hope. Neighbors resigned themselves to his care; priests gave up their incantations, and with their wives and children gratefully accepted the foreign antidote to this appalling foreign disease.

But in spite of every effort how the smallpox swept its way across the stricken island!

"During June and July when the disease was raging in our immediate neighborhood," writes Dr. Gulick, "scarce a native visited our house. Grass grew in all the paths far and wide about us, and the disease was the only topic of conversation the island round. The incessant query was for the latest reports from the various tribes as to places attacked and the number of the dead. As one and another chief of our own or some other tribe fell, the panic increased. Whole families and neighborhoods were so prostrated at once that frequently scarce an individual escaped to procure water and food of the coarsest quality for the sick; thus many died of starvation.

"The propensity was to crowd houses full; and there they lay, occupying frequently every square foot, groaning, gasping, and sweltering in the poisoned compound of air, heat, smoke, and smallpox effluvia till death released the greater number."

There was so much to do and so little time for writing, that journal records, during these months, are often nothing more than ejaculations of pity:—

"I never before was among more horrible wretchedness."

"Our hearts are rent."

"I have never before witnessed such wretched and harrowing misery."

"Such misery I never before saw, and hope never again to meet, unless I can give more efficient assistance than I find it possible now to render." And months after it was all over, ears could not forget what they had heard: —

"We still hear but too distinctly," writes Dr. Gulick, "the groaning and screeching that echoed through whole neighborhoods of breadfruit groves. We can give no adequate idea of the deadly gloom that hung over us during those dreadful months."

With the pressure of such suffering behind them the people had naturally come in increasing numbers to be inoculated; eleven one day, thirteen the next, soon twenty a day, then thirty; forty-five in a single day; one hundred and fifty-six in a week. So many crowded this surest road to life that on the fifth of August Dr. Gulick met a pathetically amusing condition of eagerness: —

"The scene was to me," he says, "a new one in my Ponape life. I found them ready and impatient to be inoculated. As I sat in the little house they crowded about the side doors, waiting their turns with impatience. They came of every age and size. Fathers and mothers brought their infants and held them firmly for me to operate on. Some of the children just old enough to be frightened shouted lustily, of course. Those of the same age, yet outdoors and about to be brought in, joined in the chorus; and these baby screechings, with the exceedingly vigorous vociferations of twenty-five or thirty adults, made a glorious din."

This is the lighter touch to a picture so dark that shadows do not show against it. On every hand, in every degree of suffering, were more who died every day than could come for inoculation; and death from smallpox in a home on Ponape meant more of pain than civilization can easily picture. In truth, this scourge is sad enough where soft sheets and gentle hands and tender nursing and Christian hope are its ministers. But on Ponape how different! Hard floor and rough mats and breathless air and hunger and ignorance and despair all seemed joined of hand to hasten their cruel fate.

And when the people died they were buried; but so many were dying every day that it was hard to bury them all; and there was such haste in burying that, half an hour after apparent death, sick bodies often rested in their crowded graves. "Buried alive sometimes," as Dr. Gulick believed; "many of them, no doubt, afterward reviving just sufficiently to pass through all the horror of a second dying."

Through these months the pathos of heathen burial appeared in each extreme; in its heartlessness was the cold brutality that wrapped an unclad, unloved body in discarded mats, thrust it into a shallow grave, filled it speedily with leaves and with earth, and danced in glee upon it; and in its hopelessness was the bitter separation from earthly clay, the newest garment tenderly wrapped about it, and the precious human casket borne by weeping friends to its resting place. There, with treasures of powder and pipe and beads and flowers, amid genuine grief and blinding tears, loving hands placed the body out of sight and gently pressed the earth upon it.

Surely human grief at parting is sad enough in any land, but saddest where there is no hope of future meeting.

Six months of dreadful history came to an end at last. And thereafter for years, as the Roman empire measured time from the building of its city, A. U. C., so history on Ponape was in sadder memory reckoned from the digging of its graves, from the era of the smallpox. Before the scourge were ten thousand merry people, physical and spiritual content, tolerance of the missionary, indifference to his message; after it five thousand bereaved human beings, half the people buried, national paralysis for a season; then spiritual restlessness, intellectual quickening, an era of awakened life — a fearful ordeal for the nation, but marking an epoch.

CHAPTER XVI.

1857.

WITH the year 1857 missionary work on Ponape reached a climax in several directions.

Months of prostration had followed the epidemic. The nation had been stunned, and life returned slowly. It was as if, trying to forget deserted places, vacant houses, and daily loneliness, the people dimly felt they might best succeed by surrendering to the new influences.

Whatever the philosophy of it, certain it is that a turning point had been reached in Ponapean history. There now sprang up an interest in reading and writing and religious teaching which surpassed anything even suggested before.

This was inspiration to the missionaries. Their efforts were redoubled. They perfected their orthographical system, hoping it would meet the needs of all Micronesian dialects. They journeyed and preached and translated, and from worn, hand-written primers still taught the people to read. Then, in 1857, Ponapean interest and American effort alike culminated in the arrival of a very small printing press.

How beautiful it was to missionary eyes! How marvelous to the embryo book-worm intelligence of Ponape! Welcome to all; but it was disappointing too, for its font was so hopelessly defective that only four small pages could be set up at a time, and this seemed slow movement to enthusiasm that had waited five years for its printing press. Joy enough was felt, however, in that at last it had come. For though none on Ponape had learned the art of printing, still the work was to be done, therefore with promptness they did it; and while eager natives waited for their primer no less eager fingers set up type and folded printed pages.

Enthusiasm is contagious even at this distance, and we turn over and over again this thin pamphlet which meant so much in 1857. Indeed, to any lover of books what can be more interesting than the first edition of the first book that is for a nation the literary stepping-stone for all that shall come after? and here it is for Micronesia: a small, blue paper-covered pamphlet of sixteen pages, each page measuring four inches by five; eight leaves neatly stitched together by hand with coarse linen thread; edges rough as modern Christmas books, but the paper itself thin and yellowed by time. Even the printer's ink is of harmonious yellow tone. So very unpretentious! Yet this small book stirred waiting Ponapeans as a new novel by George Eliot or Balzac has seldom stirred the world; and this despite contents that are to us sternly unromantic — the alphabet, a few simple phonetic spelling exercises, four pages of catechism, and four hymns. Among the latter are translations of "To-day the Saviour calls" and "There is a happy land."

This, the slender volume that trembling fingers and throbbing hearts made ready, "The Primer" that wakening intelligence welcomed with such childish delight, the first book printed in Micronesia! Happy Ponape, that with tottering steps has entered the ranks of a literary world! Happy missionaries that have materialized the intangible and made visible a language only audible before!

Native enthusiasm over the first printed page increased with each page that followed, and this interest was so genuine that students multiplied until the whole tribe was reading. Indeed, reading on Ponape in 1857 as speedily became a national enthusiasm as bicycling in the United States in 1894. It hardly seems a passing fancy, though the records show how contagious it was: —

"Our people all seem anxious to learn," writes Dr. Gulick, "and scholars are waiting about our front porch most of the time. We have now about one hundred."

"Several natives around us read everything as fast as we print."

"Went with wife to teach the Wajai and family; found them all well started through the teaching of his child. Encouraging! Thus shall the waves spread! Hope on!"

"Goliah and his three wives have commenced to read."

"We have now about one hundred and twenty scholars, including the wives of all our pilots."

"Many readers are in the second book, a few in the third."

Whatever the cause, certain it is that a new epidemic had reached Ponape. Children taught their parents, and husbands their wives. A chief built a house near Dr. Gulick to be favorably located for a course of advanced study; and though just then the Primer was the only text book, still others would soon follow, for Dr. Gulick had already translated from the Greek into Ponapean the Gospels of Matthew and John, also, separately, the Beatitudes and the Lord's Prayer.

In this work of translation Joquin had helped him — Joquin the Portuguese, the sailor, the Ponapean by adoption, the man who came to Ponape to be beyond the sound of any praying. He had been an intense sufferer for years, then a reader of the Bible that

Dr. Gulick gave him, a Christian, a friend of God, a fellow worker with the missionary, and at last, in dying, a soul that rose straight to heaven from Ponape; and when at his funeral they sang

> "There is a happy land
> Far, far away,"

the happiness of Joquin seemed more real to those who thought about it than the distance between this and the better land.

In previous years Dr. Gulick had sometimes felt discouraged, but with Joquin's Christian death and the national movement towards higher things, hope dared to breathe. And now he writes : —

"It does almost seem as though better days must be dawning — the interest is so great, though silent. Oh for the spirit of power and grace! Why may not souls be brought into the kingdom? I make it a topic of special prayer."

Then to Hawaii he wrote : "Our work has progressed. Our footing is surer. But Sebastopol is not yet taken. Our message to every Hawaiian church is: 'Pray for your mission and Micronesia, or all will fail.'"

And prayer was answered. Audiences grew. Natives began to count the days of the week from the Sabbath. They asked minutely how God was to be worshiped. They admitted his sovereignty over them

"When a Malay spoke of God as the spirit of foreign lands," writes Dr. Gulick, " a native sharply corrected him by asking if he were not equally the God of Ponape."

At the station Tulapail natives built a chapel. With roof of sago leaves and sides and floor of slender reeds it quite resembled Ponapean feasting houses. Yet there was a vital difference, for here, instead of feasting, darkened intelligence was vaguely feeling after God. Indeed, this small room, fifteen feet square, was the first church built by native hands and native contributions on Ponape.

Of the seventy people at Tulapail, forty attended church. Two alone still worshiped Ponapean spirits, and though none had yet been baptized, many claimed to be "missionaries," their synonym for Christian. On the Sabbath they neither cooked nor fished, and in their groping way they tried to keep it holy. One man said he had prayed in secret two years. A young girl, very conscientious, said she had prayed daily for a year. In view of these cases Dr. Gulick questioned the extreme conservatism of mission policy. "I sometimes query," he says, " how much more we are to require of a dark-minded heathen before admitting him to church privilege."

As yet the privilege had been granted to none. But he realized that light was shining at last. He forgot the sacrifice he had made, the life he had offered for other lives. And standing by the scales watching the weights, the balance of happiness seemed all on his side.

"What occasion for gratitude!" he exclaims. "I am stimulated to new consecration."

"This missionary life makes no subtraction from life's happiness. It is all a superaddition, a reduplication, yes, more of life's felicity. It is a substantial, real, eternal joy to kindle light in darkness, to diffuse life amidst death, to convert a wilderness to gardens, to make men of brutes, angels of men. And this is nowhere so eminently possible as where light and life have never come."

And now from this dawning light and the inspiration of it, Dr. Gulick showed the spirit that was in him by the responsibility he felt, the added sacrifice he was anxious to make for the good of Hawaiian churches. Year by year he had made careful study of Hawaiian adaptation to the different islands and dialects of Micronesia. He had also urged a closer relation between the Hawaiian churches and their foreign mission, even suggesting for them a possible independence of the American Board. And because of the nearness of the field to Hawaii and the simplicity of its language, he had urged that the Gilbert Islands be made the central point for distinctively Hawaiian missionary work. And further, as a preparation for Hawaiian work, he proposed to go thither himself as a pioneer.

"It will be more self-denying," he wrote, "than anything I have yet attempted, but so much the better! I need to have my selfishness more cut down."

"Both Louisa and I will be more than ready to go if it be thought best. My heart bounds at the thought of entering a larger field."[1]

"I wish to go. I almost feel as though I must go. We have borne the brunt of Ponape's battle; the daylight dawns; let us now, if we may, go to darker regions and there lay the foundations."

This, however, was not granted, for the need of it ended when, in this same brilliant year, 1857, the Morning Star came to Micronesia.

[1] There were 40,000 people on the Gilbert group, only 5,000 on Ponape.

CHAPTER XVII.

THE MORNING STAR.

BEFORE the Morning Star reached Ponape, church history in America had been made richer by its chapter on the love of the children that built and sent her. That history cannot wholly be omitted here.

In 1855 the Micronesian Mission had made formal request for a mission schooner. In the same year also, as if moved by the same impulse, Secretaries, planning in Boston, decided to build a vessel of one hundred and fifty tons, to cost twelve thousand dollars, to be called the Morning Star. A happy thought suggested that the children be asked to build her. Shares were therefore offered at ten cents apiece; and certificates of stock were neatly engraved and issued in very formal fashion. They testified that Mary or Susan or James had taken a specified number of shares in the Morning Star.

Youthful interest was at once secured, and Christian children rallied to build their missionary packet. In America boys ran on errands and denied themselves luxuries; girls hemmed pocket handkerchiefs and saved their dimes; fathers and mothers were enlisted;

friends were importuned; while multitudes of children dreamed of their Morning Star and loved her. To many boys and girls the height of earthly ambition was a hope some day to sail, in this ship of theirs, to distant mystic Micronesia.

The interest spread to other lands. Turkish children saved half-cents from their poverty, and Chinese children, with slender yellow fingers, tenderly counted their "cash." A Sunday-school on the Hawaiian Islands sent fifty dollars, "every penny of it earned," as was claimed, "by the toil of the children's hands." Some of that toiling was done in the fields before daylight, when the moon was shining and the inspiring morning star itself also glowing in the sky.

Money poured into the treasury. Shares were first taken in August, 1855; and the figures of receipts are significant of the spreading interest. In August, $34.68; in September, $886.98; in October, $5,763.28; in November, $10,710. In fact, as reported at the time, "Coppers and three-cent pieces and half-dimes came in by quarts if not by gallons." More than enough had been raised, but still the children gave. Children in Canada, in India, in Africa were soon giving; and a year after the keel was laid 285,454 shares had been taken. The Morning Star had cost $13,000, and the remaining $15,000 were kept for insurance and repairs.

In November, 1856, four thousand people had gathered to see her launched. Over half of them were children who had come to see the work their pennies had done; and eyes that glistened as these young stockholders walked about with an air of conscious ownership showed how pleased the children were. Indeed, from fore to aft, from shining keel to slender mast, how the value of invested pennies revealed itself to them! To cap the climax of youthful enthusiasm, were four flags that floated gayly above them — two from each mast. One carried the name Morning Star. Under it was the white flag of peace. From the mainmast streamed the Stars and Stripes, and below it was the private signal — a white star on a background of blue.

Childish hearts breathed a sigh of content. They had certainly invested wisely; and as their graceful craft glided from the stocks into the waters of Chelsea, the small shareholders shouted with delight. But there were tears in the eyes of the older people.

Five months later other shareholders welcomed the Morning Star with equal delight to Honolulu. "*Nani*," they said; "*nani loa*" (very beautiful). And they too sped her on with the breath of prayer.

And then, on the twenty-fourth of September, she was welcomed, words cannot tell how welcomed, by the Christians on Ponape. Perhaps no inanimate thing was ever more tenderly loved by human beings than this Morning Star by missionaries in Micronesia. Before she came they loved her; and while, for two months, they waited for her every day, their love for her steadily grew; and when she reached them a broader band of sunlight followed her to Micronesia than had ever been seen there before.

Dr. Gulick had gone out to meet this stranger craft whose flags could surely not deceive him. As he drew near to her side, his father waited upon her deck to greet him. There too was his brother Orramel. Mr. and Mrs. Snow were also there from Kusaie, while, standing broad-shouldered and high among them, was his childhood's playfellow, Hiram Bingham. He too had come as a missionary to Micronesia. It was not long before they were all gathered in the thatched cottage at Shalong, where the first and instinctive expression of their grateful hearts was in prayer. The terrible isolation was at last broken. A highway opened by the hands of children bound Micronesia to the world again. "Easy now," as Dr. Gulick says, "to forget all the loneliness of the past, when we think of the ten thousand little owners following her like guardian spirits with their prayers and sympathies. God bless the Morning Star! God bless her owners!"

Mr. and Mrs. Doane had come to Micronesia in 1855. Mr. and Mrs. Bingham had now joined the mission for the Gilbert Islands. And these all, with the Hawaiian missionaries and Mr. and Mrs. Sturges from Rono Kiti, met at Shalong and exchanged mutual help and stimulus.

But the time had come to separate. It was October 16, 1857. The Morning Star was about to take the missionaries back to their scattered fields and to their isolation. Besides the missionaries, she would take from Dr. Gulick his father and his brother who had come to visit him. Not only this, but, for the sake of her health, there would also sail away on the Morning Star his wife and his two children — all the world for him at Shalong Point. Where loneliness had reigned before for the family, sterner loneliness than ever now faced the individual.

Five o'clock in the afternoon; the sun burning its way to the horizon; two miles outside the reef; a sea that is growing rough; Dr. Gulick can go with them no farther. Therefore with words that choke him and eyes that cannot see, he leaves the Morning Star, and in his frail canoe, through gathering shadows and deepening twilight, he returns to wait through the loneliness of another year for the coming again of his dear ones.

Heathen darkness around him and no light in his home! but God still in his heaven, and a sure conviction with him still that all is wisely ordered. Thus he trusts the Lord as he sits alone in the empty house and writes of his submission : —

"I cannot expect to see all those dear ones again till this life is merged in eternal day. But we bow before Him who is preëminently the bright and Morning Star."

CHAPTER XVIII.

WAITING.

THE following ten months passed slowly at Shalong, though an old family servant from Hawaii was installed in the kitchen. It were well indeed to have food and a cook to prepare it for him, yet " since the Morning Star left," writes Dr. Gulick, "my heart has been wandering over the waste of waters without a home."

But he hoped the change would do his wife good and "make her," as he says, " the same brave, strong, vigorous, demurely roguish girl I so unceremoniously married six years ago, and with whom I have floated through many a honeymoon on Ponape." Then, continuing about his wife, he tells us that " she has great physical energy and freedom from fear;" that " she is one of the most heavenly minded of Christians — my constant instructor and mentor. Since she left me," he adds, " I have stolen the reading of her private journals from early girlhood, and my soul feels itself poor in the Christian life beside her."

Now, however, life moved on without her, and Dr. Gulick suffered in every way.

"I please only myself nowadays," he writes; "I retire to sleep at all hours as the whim takes me, from seven P.M. to one or two A.M. I usually rise at six. I eat two meals a day and no lunch. Sometimes I breakfast at seven, sometimes at ten o'clock, and my dinner is masticated at any time from three to seven P.M."

Add to this irregularity the sense of isolation which seldom left him, which drove him to much overdoing, and the depression that came later explains itself.

"If a man can feel thus forlorn," he wrote to his wife, "what must a woman suffer! what must you suffer! It seems to grow more and more unbearable!"

Yet after all there was nothing to do but to endure, to keep busy and brave, and to wait. And while he waited a new necessity came to him.

Enterprising leaders in Ponapean society had, even in 1856, begun to wear imported garments and sigh for imported styles. As a result Mrs. Gulick had joyfully cut out calico dresses and taught the women to sew. Now during her absence, a sudden whirl of desire for foreign-made garments laid hold of many other women, and Dr. Gulick was called on to design and cut out this clothing for them. He quietly tried to influence them toward the simple Mother Hubbard gown worn on Hawaii; but to Ponapean eyes this was not modern enough. They expressly desired tight-fitting dresses, such as Mrs. Gulick and Mrs. Sturges wore. There was no escape and Dr. Gulick added one more accomplishment to his growing list. For weeks now he was a lady's tailor.

He found Mrs. Gulick's patterns — one large, the other small — and by a quick mental estimate in the case of each applicant decided which to use. There could not well be any variation from the pattern, for Dr. Gulick was not by instinct a dressmaker.

This fever was well advanced by May, 1858, and lasted four months. The following are some of the symptoms of its progress: —

"I was all day yesterday making dresses. We had five under way at once. Strange work for a man!"

"Making dresses all this week. I shall be curious to know whether you approve the way in which they fit. The set of sleeves is that in which I most completely fail."

"Have to-day cut out three boys' shirts, one woman's sack, and two petticoats, and superintended sewing all day. I begin to feel almost ready for the Morning Star. When will you come!"

"Within two months have made about twenty dresses, besides having disposed of more than as many more readymade dresses and slips. When the Morning Star comes we mean to make a grand display of our finery, for we propose having a sort of jubilee over her return, to be celebrated by all who have dresses! Our piety is fully as deep, I think, as the mass of that in New York. I have sold all the calico sent for sale, disposed of all the readymade dresses I could find, and at last laid hold on all the odd pieces and remnants and choice patterns my wife had stored away in her drawers and chests. I don't know what she will think about it. I only know she will not scold much."

The whole tide of this mania is so amusing that one almost forgets the affliction it was to Dr. Gulick. He wanted to study the language more scientifically, to continue his translating and his work on the Ponape vocabulary. But for months he was hindered somewhat by this other imperative requirement. Nothing, however, ever really prevented mental work. Other duties simply drove him to press the harder; to crowd sleep into very small compass; to fill days so full that exercise and eating were left to chance adjustment. At this time, indeed, he wrote and studied and preached as seldom before. Letters to The Missionary Herald were his contribution to the life of American churches; and letters to brothers and friends were the more potent personal influence.

For his own sake Dr. Gulick longed for friends; and the practice of intimate letter-writing in Micronesia emphasized his early tendencies, making still more fixed his habit of reticence. For thereafter, through life, much to his regret, he was as a rule more reserved in personal conversation with his friends than in his correspondence with them.

"I have no special messages of love to write," he once wrote to his mother; "I only wish to tell you I love you. I fear your heart was pained on my return from the States by my coldness of exterior. I am sometimes troubled by this thought, yet how could I be otherwise? During all my American life I had no mother; I had no brother or sister. This made me naturally reserved. I may never see you again on earth, but in heaven, if I ever get there, I shall be different. I shall be all you can desire."

As if by some charm of his pen, distance was banished when Dr. Gulick wrote his letters. The far-off friend was beside him again and they talked together, and this quiet talking in the library on Ponape was heard in many places. Through it his boyhood's friend, Hiram Bingham, had already come to Micronesia, and reached by it fresh life and quickened zeal came to the Hawaiian churches and to the Hawaiian Mission Children's Society that supported him.

"My soul glows with excitement," he wrote, "as I think of the future day when the members of our society shall be scattered along on all the isles of Micronesia, in Malaysia, in China, in Japan, among the Indians of Kamskatka and Oregon, and along the Spanish Main! How pleasant will it be to ascend from these various fields to meet about our Saviour's throne! How pleasant to feel and know that we have thus fulfilled our Saviour's purpose!"

The truth is, it had not occurred to Dr. Gulick to consider his mission field as bounded by the shores of Ponape or the islands of Micronesia; and so, sitting in the silence of Shalong, remote and alone, he reached out with unflagging zeal to encourage others. Thus it was that through those buried years on Ponape he proved hardly less a missionary to America and Hawaii than to Micronesia itself.

But while he helped his friends his own need increased. This is best seen in a daily journal kept for his wife alone. Too personal for large quotation here, a few items must suffice to show his approaching nervous prostration: —

"I have to-day had a touch of my old malady. I had the same weight at my heart, the same forlorn desire for sympathy that was the incubus of my youth. I had forgotten what woeful sensations they were. What an awful six years should I have spent had you not taken pity on me!"

"Intellectual effort of late brings on painful aching in my head, which will, I fear, yet prevent my studying much, an affliction I must seek grace to endure."

"Do not feel strong."

"Is my relish for reading and study abating?"

"I would often like to escape from this condition of existence. It seems to me at such times that I should be much better adapted to usefulness if relieved of this physique. Still, the fact that life will, at the longest, soon be gone, moderates this feeling; and then occasionally — occasionally — the hope that I may, after all, accomplish somewhat for the cause of holiness makes my whole horizon flash with a light which must be akin to that irradiating heaven."

"I got so lonely this afternoon that I brought your family portrait and set it up at the head of my desk."

"It horrifies me to tell you that thoughts of suicide will every once and a while float through my brain. Oh, this life without you is fast using me up! Shall I ever get back to where I have been in tolerable degree of cheerfulness?"

"What a whirl my head and heart are in! Your letters arrived this morning! Need I say more?"

"I am sinking down, down, in mind and body here. If death would only release me, how happy!"

"Saw the Morning Star this morning in my sleep."

"I often wonder whether I am ever to see you again. Perhaps you are already in the spirit land! Joy for you, but inexpressible sorrow for me!"

"I begin to wonder if some accident has not overtaken the Morning Star. You may be suffering. I will pray for you; it is all I can do."

"A small speck was seen this afternoon. What joy should it be the Morning Star and you and our children! What an abyss of sorrow should any of you not be on the Morning Star! I long yet dread to know the whole."

It was the Morning Star. Weeks and months of waiting were ended now. Once more in Shalong, in the library where one alone had spent the months, wife and children were again gathered to him, and while Dr. Gulick poured out a thankful heart in prayer, his wife, still young, kneeling beside him, could not restrain her tears of joy.

But the children on land again merrily danced about and wondered why their mother should cry when they were so very happy.

CHAPTER XIX.

THE CLOSE OF HIS LIFE IN MICRONESIA.

THE Morning Star came and went once a year. During its presence, and by means of it, the mission, growing slowly, met in general meeting. They discussed vital problems — the adaptability of Hawaiian missionaries to the work; the needs of different islands; the possibility of most usefulness on each; the health of the missionaries; the required appropriations for the different stations. And when the conference ended the mission kaleidoscope was often well shaken.

In 1859, of American missionaries there were Mr. and Mrs. Snow still on Kusaie; Mr. and Mrs. Sturges with Mr. and Mrs. Roberts on Ponape; Mr. and Mrs. Bingham on Apaiang, of the Gilbert Islands; Mr. and Mrs. Doane and Dr. and Mrs. Gulick on Ebon, of the Marshall Islands; while Dr. and Mrs. Pierson were returning to America in broken health.

There was no great dissimilarity in the experiences of the missionaries on the different islands. Indeed, the life of Dr. Gulick on Ponape may be held fairly to represent the life of other missionaries at that time in Micronesia. Each, of necessity, was individual in the line of greatest personal suffering; but, for all, there was physical discomfort, hard work, ignorant people, tired nerves, isolation. And under such pressure the more nervous failed soonest.

It had been hoped that for Dr. Gulick life on Ebon might stimulate his health, worn low on Ponape. Then, too, Mr. and Mrs. Doane needed him medically.

He had gone, hoping to spend yet many years in Micronesia. This, however, was not to be.

The work was now well started. Progress was reported everywhere. The movement at Ponape with Dr. Gulick and Mr. Sturges had been but part of the whole. The regular coming of the Morning Star brought new life to all. It made loneliness and hardship easier to bear. It seemed a proof that love and strength in larger places had not forgotten the smallness of Micronesia.

But there came one year an astonishment, under which even missionary devotion caught its breath. The Morning Star itself brought the proposition. It suggested a possible sale of the Morning Star, and abandonment of the work in Micronesia. The reasons for this were the expense of the mission; the smallness of the field; the hardships endured by its missionaries; the growing interest of the Hawaiian churches in their nearer mission, the Marquesas Islands, and last, but most real, the pecuniary embarrassment of the American Board.

Fancy might easily imagine that a sigh of relief would have come to tired missionaries at the prospect of honorable release from this hard life, or at least that their plea for Micronesia would not include any suggestion of willingness to endure more of privation than had already come to them; yet not so.

The mission had gathered in its annual meeting. Dr. Gulick was appointed scribe; and as Abraham pleaded once for Sodom, so he now in behalf of the mission pleads for Micronesia. In watching the patient courage of this man it is hard to keep back the tears. Pale now and worn; tormented by headache; older than his years, he is yet seriously offering his life and the life of this mission in exchange for the life of Micronesia. The argument covers many pages. At its close is the summary : —

"We then turn each objection into an argument, and urge the continuance of our mission because it is not much more expensive than other missions; because, being small, it may be hoped it may bring rapid returns; because the field is, in the main, so favorable to our health and comfort; because the continuance of the American part of our mission is so essential to the drawing of Hawaiian energies to Micronesia; because, notwithstanding the Board's embarrassment, the abandonment will be so disastrous to the cause of missions at home, to our poor people, and to our own usefulness."

In addition this plea begs that the Morning Star be not withdrawn from them. But if in spite of their asking she should be removed, what then? Will missionaries sail out over the horizon with her and never come back again to Micronesia? Without wavering the mission recalls that previous isolation and yet answers: "Should she be removed, we beg to be allowed to labor as we did before she came." And this is so sincerely their wish that to make its granting more possible to home Christians they add an inducement to it. They will try, they say, to reduce expenses, to economize more, to deny themselves things that have seemed necessities heretofore.

They make no suggestion of economy to those friends at home who, on soft cushions in dimly shaded churches, find it difficult sometimes to drop their dimes and their dollars into velvet contribution bags and silver plates. Neither do they tell them that in Micronesia missionaries already live in simplicity that would appall most Christian economy at home. Without a thought of the sarcasm that might have been breathed into it they make this proposition of a stricter economy for themselves.

But what if even this avail not? Shall Micronesia

then be left to perish as Sodom? Nay, of that one impossibility they have no question. And therefore, still writing calmly, they add: —

"If the Board is unable to support even ourselves without the Morning Star, we shall ask the privilege of helping ourselves in what business we can, rather than desert Micronesia."

Even missionary heroism had reached its limit now. There was nothing more to offer. Yet in faded writing on the yellow pages there are still these other words: "Our hearts quiver as we ask if we, our people, and our cause have so lost our hold on American churches as to make them wish to recall us, or even to consent to it?"

Who could resist such an appeal? Surely not Secretaries in Boston nor Christian churches that, in spite of apparent coldness sometimes, did, after all, believe in their missionaries, in the Morning Star, and in their work in Micronesia. From that day to this the Morning Star has visited Micronesia once a year. Not the same packet now as then, for one has been replaced by another until now the fourth in line of that first Morning Star is helped by steam. And missionaries to-day, with reasonable hope of regularity, plan for the coming of what is still the most welcome sight in Micronesia — the blessed Morning Star.

The change to Ebon had effected little for Dr.

Gulick physically. His vitality was already too thoroughly sapped. At length even brave determination yielded. Yet the thought of return to life and the world again was now a dread and not a delight. He shrank from its intensity.

"The idea of meeting the formalities of 'society' unnerves me," he writes. "The truth is I am about used up. I have lost much of my relish for society, for conversation. It is with effort I maintain any tolerable degree of sociability. I am nearly useless as a missionary. The prostration of my nervous system makes it necessary that I take a vacation; and consequently our six stations on five different islands where five American and four Hawaiian families are stationed along a line of a thousand miles are left without a physician."

In October, 1860, the Morning Star returned to Honolulu; and with her she brought Dr. Gulick, his wife, his children, and his books — the things he loved. Household possessions were left in Micronesia, for he expected to return to them.

And now he is welcomed again to the land of his birth and to his father's house. God seemed very kind. But showing what those nine years in Micronesia had done for Dr. Gulick, the simple entry is: "He is so changed that no one recognizes him."

CHAPTER XX.

CHANGES.

EVEN with its delight of friends and horseback riding and civilized comforts again, life on Hawaii did not bring health to Dr. Gulick. He was sent to the Marquesas Islands as delegate from the Hawaiian churches to their mission there; yet neither did this avail. Then he went to California; and this touching again of home shores was the beginning of a new era in his life. Through it he gained a reputation as an electric missionary speaker which never left him. At last he realized the ambition of his passionate, aspiring youth. He reached people and moved them by the power of his public speaking.

The opening of this era was in San Francisco. Through courtesy to his missionary calling he had been asked to address a Sunday-school. It was a simple talk about Micronesia and the Morning Star, yet the children who listened to him awakened suddenly to an actual belief in foreign missions and heathen people and a world which they might touch, though they never saw it.

Soon he bought a California pony and on this small creature visited various towns. To increase his Micronesian salary and to gain practice in speaking English again he sometimes gave public lectures. In one place " I gave a boy a ticket and a half dollar," he writes, " to go about town ringing a bell and shouting about the lecture. I had an audience of perhaps forty-five. I talked for an hour and a half and interested all. Expenses four dollars; receipts nine dollars; profits five dollars."

At another time he cleared forty-five dollars. Still later:—

" Spoke to the children of the academy, perhaps one hundred and fifty. Produced uproarious laughter and some cheering. I do not please myself in this matter," he adds. " It is hard for me to be interesting without provoking laughter. I pray for grace to assist me. May my sins be pardoned!"

A touch of pathos, for his audience had probably gone home and thanked the Lord for this brilliant, godly, human missionary who made them laugh and cry by turns.

With this power of his he stirred alike Sunday-schools and churches, aroused interest, and secured large pledges of help for Micronesia. But his head still troubled him. Friends argued against any return to foreign missionary work, and physicians declared that at least Micronesia was out of the question. He was himself greatly perplexed.

"I am," he says, "at the turning point of my life. By one step now I can very nearly decide for all the future against continuing any form of foreign missionary life. Shall I take it? My only wish is to follow the indications of Providence. I care not what they are."

He measured himself, indeed, when he found it "harder to decide not to be a missionary than to decide to be one." And for this reason, no less than to postpone immediate decision, he took passage for the Eastern states — took it "with almost a shudder," as he says, "to think how near I came to a termination of my missionary life by stopping here."

With this ultimate question unanswered, therefore, he reached New York. It was September, 1862.

In October he attended the meeting of the American Board in Springfield, Mass., and began at once what appears to have been his missionary conquest of the Eastern churches. He was encouraged when missionary fathers whom he honored assured him "that he spoke much better than the mass of returned missionaries," and further strengthened when pastors sent word to each other that "Dr. Gulick would electrify them all."

His addresses were largely extempore, and we can

only measure them now by the effect they produced then. Certain it is, however, that the enthusiasm which followed them was as a rising tide, and that this enthusiasm was mental and physical tonic to Dr. Gulick. To appreciate this we must remember that since he was twenty-four — and now he was thirty-four — he had struggled for breath in the heavy mental atmosphere of Micronesia, and that he was now abruptly introduced into intellectual ozone.

This public speaking was continuous from October, 1862, until August, 1863. Sometimes he traveled and spoke with other missionaries at church conventions. Sometimes he went alone to Sunday-schools and churches that needed him. While "everywhere," as he tells his wife, "I am the recipient of all the kindness and attention I could desire. It is very pleasant to find myself in demand publicly," he adds, "improving to my mind and invigorating to my spirits."

Audiences were at first attracted by the new topic — the first missionary who had come back to them from what had seemed another world. Soon, however, the man himself magnetized them. Larger numbers came to hear him and meetings each day were multiplied. First one and two, then two and three, and after that sometimes five and six engagements in a single day!

This was appalling, and yet it inspired him. He

grew tired but not exhausted. With Micronesian stagnation behind him, his hunger for people and for action needed much, perhaps, to satisfy it. Indeed, "I dread inaction," he wrote to Mr. Treat, "yet occasionally I have done a little too much." Letters to his wife prove this : —

"Have spoken six times to-day, in all about three hours and ten minutes. Of course I am tired, but am gaining strength." "Spoke four times on Wednesday in Andover." "In Hartford spoke to a crowded house of adults and many children, the largest missionary meeting, I am told, they have had since the meeting of the Board here years ago."

Sometimes there were rival efforts to secure him, as in February, when, as he writes, "There was quite a struggle between the agents of the Park Street and Charlestown churches regarding me for their Sabbath-school concerts next Sabbath. It is decided in favor of Park Street."

And this, though he had already been there twice. As a result, "Spent Saturday night in Malden, and preached there in the morning. Rode two miles to Melrose and preached. A carriage came for me, and I rode eight miles to Boston, and under the influence of a cracking headache spoke to a crowded vestry in Park Street Church with more than usual liveliness and effect! Feel Mondayish to-day!"

Perhaps Park Street Church felt a sense of ownership in him, for he had previously reminded them of the fact that thirty-five years before, in this same missionary-spirited church, his father had received instruction from the officers of the Board as a missionary to Hawaii; and that now, for eleven years, in the foreign mission of that mission, children of those missionaries and converts of that mission had been working side by side as foreign missionaries in Micronesia.

From Boston Dr. Gulick went to Maine. And here older folks and children too came through blinding snowstorms to hear him.

In truth the children always felt as if this man whose prayers they had helped to answer belonged peculiarly to them, this missionary who had begged for the Morning Star and prayed for her, and waited for her and sailed in her, and who now told them all about her. What wonder that many came to hear him? And what wonder that, moved by his power, those children went home and drew out their certificates of stock in the Morning Star, and counted themselves richer than they had dreamed, and resolved that they too would some day be this splendid thing, a foreign missionary to Micronesia!

And so the call was constant from church to church, from town to town, until a rapid summary in March gives us a glimpse of the pressure he was under : —

"In twenty-two days I have spoken forty-three times in sixteen different places scattered through three different states. I must rest as much as I can in three or four days, and then start off for western New York, to be gone a month."

While he kept thus busy, it is interesting to watch his struggle towards higher ideals in speaking. Dissatisfaction came to him through a certain gift of his. His audiences laughed too much!

Laughter was well sometimes, as at that Congregational gathering where " Dr. Stearns, of Amherst, Drs. Buddington, Beecher, several others, and I were," as he tells us, " ' the organ grinders of fun,' " and where " I believe I did my share, I, the long-faced, melancholy missionary!" But the trouble was that even church audiences were constantly wreathed in smiles. In fact, the serious boy, the lonely, consecrated missionary to Micronesia, suddenly surprised himself no less than his friends by being a wit now in America; and his rebuke to himself was that church audiences were not left by him in more serious mood.

"Preached in Chelsea, in Mr. Plumb's pulpit. Was not so solemn as I ought to have been."

"Spoke once in the morning and twice in the afternoon, quite outdoing myself in producing laughter, but not leaving the best results."

"My last address at East Concord was a wonder to myself in the amusement it produced. How I fail in coming up to what I desire!"

But there still remained the old power of self-conquest; and as a result we again read: —

"I am being helped to develop the spiritual aspects of our mission work. The Lord guide me!"

"My utmost desires are gratified. All the dreamings of my life are being realized."

At the same time also items of approval found their way into daily papers: —

"A picture talk." "Rare descriptive power." "Thrilling sketches of original heathenism." "An eloquent and impassioned speaker." "One of the most eloquent men of the day."

One young man wrote to another: "For power as a preacher, for plainness, point, and eloquence, I am not acquainted with his equal. If he wants the world to appreciate his talents, he had better turn his back on Micronesia where the returns are so slow, the rewards so far in the future."

Similar suggestion came often to him.

The great war of the rebellion still continued; and Dr. Gulick's letters are constantly threaded with his interest in every move the armies made. Yet through all this, through his flashings of humor and pathos, through the smiles of his audience and their tears, there was never any question as to the power that moved him most. It was always his devotion to the heathen world — to Hawaii and to Micronesia. He counted himself only a missionary at home on a furlough.

In harmony with this and by special request of Dr. Anderson, who was about to visit Hawaii, Dr. Gulick made a full written statement of what the needs there seemed to him to be.[1] This was approved in Boston, and speaking of him at this time the venerable senior Secretary of the Board said: "Dr. Gulick has better views of the working of missions than any young man I have ever met."

The question of return to Micronesia had by this time answered itself. Dr. Gulick was not physically able to undertake it. Moreover, in August, 1863, he was invited to return to Honolulu as secretary of the recently organized Board of the Hawaiian Evangelical Association.

His cherished desire seemed to be increasingly fulfilled, for now he should work most directly for foreign

---

[1] The points he makes are the need of efficient foreign ministers in the central stations; the need of new and interesting books; the need of a native pastorate; the need of girls' schools, and the need of an efficient ecclesiastical organization. He also proposed that the Hawaiian churches have more responsibility; that there be but one missionary organization on the Islands and that that one be representative of the churches.

missions from the vantage ground of his dearly loved Hawaii.

"What occasion have I to bless the Lord!" he exclaims. "Was a man ever more completely delivered out of all his troubles!" For us the exclamation is: "Ah, the blessedness of human inability to peer into the future!" Yet even for him there were forebodings of trial in "the anxiety that increases upon me;" in the "shrinking from the bare anticipation;" in the prayer to be "saved from indiscretion," to be granted "wisdom to press into every duty."

"It sometimes seems," he says, "as though I could not bear up under the great pressure of the position. My shoulders and my soul ache in advance." But the journey had been made. Hawaii was near to him again. And now writing to his wife:—

"We are rocking in a calm when my heart wishes we were flying on the wings of a gale."

"You already are expecting me and every vessel that comes makes you almost sick with excitement. But all will be lost in joy when we meet."

Dr. Gulick reached Honolulu on the seventh of January, 1864; and this is his prayer: "Lord, help me in the work before me. Keep me near thyself."

CHAPTER XXI.

THE NEW WORK.

CHRISTIAN work on the Hawaiian Islands was in a state of evolution when Dr. Gulick joined it in 1864. The thing to be evolved was a self-supporting native ministry.

In some respects it seems cause for astonishment that after forty-three years of unrelenting missionary effort there should have been in 1863 but four Hawaiian pastors of the twenty-one native churches of the Islands. This appears the more strange when we know that, in larger proportion than in the United States, the people could at that time read and write and had acquaintance with the running outline of Bible story.

Two facts are, however, the easy explanation of the situation. In the first place, to missionaries who had taught them there had not as yet seemed sufficient strength of character in this childlike Hawaiian people to justify the placing of any large independent responsibility upon them. Veteran missionaries still remained, therefore, the pastors of the people; and their parishes were often fifty and sixty miles in length.

In the second place, it was not the practice of the American Board in any of its foreign missions to press native converts rapidly into pastoral work.[1] In following out this policy, however, the mission realized in 1863 that a crisis was upon them and that, unless something immediate and radical were done, the result would mean sad undoing of the work into which they had woven their lives. If death were not so stern a master, so inexorable, the crisis might have been postponed indefinitely; but in point of fact the missionaries were already growing old, and no younger men were being sent to fill their places. What should be done to supply the need when weight of years should bear the older men out of sight?

This question was met and answered at the annual meeting of the Evangelical Association of 1863, Dr. Anderson being present as Secretary from the American Board.

Under the circumstances there would seem to have been but one answer possible, which by common consent was promptly given. Church responsibility must be thrown at once upon the Hawaiians themselves, and this while American missionaries still lived to help them with their counsel. The Hawaiians were certainly neither so strong nor so able as their fathers in Israel,

[1] "Nor was this peculiar to the Sandwich Islands. At that time only thirty-eight of the one hundred and seventy churches connected with the American Board had native pastors." — *Dr. Anderson.*

the missionaries; but, since the matter had practically reduced itself to a choice of evils, the wisdom of the mission decided in favor of having the Hawaiians practice walking alone in church work while older pedestrians could still be summoned for emergencies.[1]

To accomplish this, various revolutionary measures were adopted, as the admission of Hawaiian pastors, delegates, and missionaries to full membership with the American missionaries in the Evangelical Association; the use of the Hawaiian instead of the English language in its meetings; the formation of Island Associations[2] which "were to organize churches, define territorial limits, ordain and install pastors," etc.

But reaching the matter most vitally perhaps was the resolve to urge Hawaiian young men to prepare for pastoral work;[3] the missionaries practically pledging themselves to a division and subdivision of their fields as fast as Hawaiians should be found to take the churches.

Now all this was in some respects as a grant of

[1] Though weakness appeared among the native pastors, as had been anticipated, still when the fathers died their places were better filled than if during their lifetime Hawaiians had not already borne full church responsibility. As one who has spent his life on Hawaii has expressed it: "We should have been wrecked long since but for those changes. The new era brought the only possible salvation."

[2] These organizations were called Associations or Presbyteries, according to the will of the majority in each place. The work they did was the same. One only was called a Presbytery — that on Maui.

[3] With no churches to be supplied, Hawaiians had in the past neither sought nor in general been urged to seek full preparation for this work.

suffrage to the people. Heretofore they had been as children in church government. Mission fathers had answered all difficult problems for them; but now these same fathers seemed to say: "To-day you are men. To-day you begin to vote. Acquit you like men, and let us always help you when we can."

To further share responsibility with them, a Board was appointed by this same epoch-making Association of 1863 called "The Board of the Hawaiian Evangelical Association." It comprised eighteen members, six of whom were Hawaiians. It was to meet twice a month, and here too the Hawaiian and not the English language was used. This Hawaiian Board was of necessity the heart of the General Association. In it were centered all church and benevolent interests whether at home or abroad; and through it the American Board did its work both on Hawaii and in Micronesia. Indeed, in a real sense the American Board, so far as this work in the Pacific was involved, made itself at this time auxiliary to the Hawaiian Board. It was eagerly helping Hawaii to walk alone as a mission.

The new craft was certainly well laden. Practically the first of Hawaiian mission children to become a foreign missionary had been called to be its captain.[1]

---

[1] William Richards, who died on reaching China, was the first one to go out under appointment as a missionary.

Enough of introduction, that, with Micronesia behind him, Dr. Gulick was not in danger of bringing added burdens to Hawaiian foreign missionaries by experimental application of homemade theories. He was not to try the strange experiment of unfastening heathen chains with hands which had not been quite brave enough to touch the heathen themselves. A Hawaiian; a missionary; a man who thought problems through and, regardless of self, tried to do his part in answering them, — this was Dr. Gulick who had come back to the help of Hawaii.

Yet the very fact of his Hawaiian birth and intimacy with mission questions had served to heighten his appreciation of the difficulties before him. He knew that even consecrated humanity is, after all, human, and that it would be a hard thing for veteran leaders in large parishes to resign the work of their lives to the hands of natives who were, at best, inferior to themselves in strength of character, in mental discipline, in experience; and that when it came to the actual point of parish division godly men might hesitate and seriously question whether the interests of Zion did not demand the continued resting of their hands upon the ark. But Dr. Gulick had come to Hawaii with all this in view.

A special meeting of the Board was held on the twelfth of February, 1864, to welcome him to his work.

"Pleasant, satisfactory," he says, "my initiation. The Lord be praised! The Lord guide and direct!"

Then the practical work of organization began; and at once he found himself "swimming in deep waters without a precedent" to guide him. "Yet much seems to be expected of me," he writes. In truth, what the Board was to the association, that was its executive officer to the Board — its heart and soul. It was for him to start movements which should carry out its large plans; and, once started, he was to see that these plans were executed. Besides this there were the multiplied routine duties which fell to him as both Home and Foreign Secretary — annual reports, statistical tables, and constant communication with Secretaries in Boston, with all parts of Hawaii, and with each missionary in Marquesas and the Micronesian Islands.

Such were the requirements of his office, and how can one even outline the effort he made to fulfill them all! For months at first he was traveling and counseling with the missionaries and organizing Island Associations and meeting the natives; then there were native pastors to be ordained, large parishes to be made smaller, churches to be organized, and through it all the hearty coöperation of most of those for whom he acted.

But as in all radical movements, so in this: there

was the conservative balance wheel in constant revolution. Thus it appears, for he tells us that "the radical independence of Congregationalism stands among us with swords drawn ready to slash and shout to New England sectarianism for help against the iniquitous ecclesiastical system into which the Hawaiian churches fell in 1863."

In face of its own previous action this same conservative wheel revolved in some dismay over the question of parish division. Indeed, it appears as a curious fact that a certain few of the older missionaries seem to have believed strenuously in the principle of a native pastorate for the parish of their neighbor, while as strenuously resisting the application of the same principle to their own fields.

"For me to enter these fields in my capacity of Home Secretary," writes Dr. Gulick, "would be the signal for the exercise of the severest of broomsticks. Between all these elements therefore," he adds, " I have to step carefully." For him, however, careful stepping did not mean the ceasing to walk altogether. On the contrary, he took such rapid steps that by the last of 1864 he had been "received with kindness by all," was "greatly encouraged," and was able to report: —

"The associations of the island of Hawaii have arranged for twenty-four evangelical church organizatious, nineteen of them to be under native ministers. Eight of these nineteen are already organized with pastors, while four others are for the present year supplied with licensed pastors."

However important his own share in this work, Dr. Gulick nevertheless claimed little for himself. "For years," he tells us, "the fathers of Hawaii have been preparing the way for this very step; we are now but seeing the fruit."

Still we to-day realize, as his co-workers did, that results so suddenly in advance of all anticipation signify the presence of one who was a genius in organizing forces and marshaling men. In point of fact, this gift as a leader seems to have been increasingly through life the possession of Dr. Gulick; so much so that in speaking of him twenty years later an aged missionary said: "Yes; we all worked together with him. No, not together; he was a king among us."

As for the Hawaiians themselves, they were devotedly his friends, both because of frequent tours among them and even more perhaps through the growing interest of his newspaper, The Kuokoa, or Independent — so independent sometimes that it soon brought much trial with it! Of this Kuokoa Dr. Gulick became proprietor and editor[1] on the first of

---

[1] For a season the Rev. H. H. Parker was a fellow editor with him.

January, 1865, and the undertaking proved what he had anticipated — "a post of great and incessant labor." He assumed it "because it is in the line of my official duties and because it will greatly increase my influence and contact with the natives."

Nor had he overestimated either the toil involved in editing it or the influence which this paper would exert. It was for the Hawaiians both a missionary and a literary magazine, no less than a religious newspaper and political bulletin; and this because there was, when it first appeared, no other weekly newspaper printed in the native language. In it, therefore, all varieties of interest were centered. Here were association reports; accounts of installations; news from foreign missions, from America and the world; discussion of vital home questions; advice, warning, and encouragement.

Through it all pastors no less than other people recognized one avowed high purpose — the good of Hawaii. When, therefore, The Kuokoa came to them once a week they welcomed it as a personal friend; and when the editor himself took them by the hand and said "*Aloha*,"[1] their love for him was very real.

They often proved this by their hospitality, for no hotels waited near the scattered churches when he toured among them. The home of the missionary

[1] "Love to you."

Luther Halsey Gulick

was often far away, but *Kauka Kulika*[1] was always welcomed by the native pastor. When he came, sun-browned children with coal-black eyes scampered off to tell their friends that *Kauka Kulika* had come, while the quiet hostess spread her simple meal of poi and fish with much apology. But poi and fish were feast enough for Hawaiian of any shade. Therefore before it there was the blessing and after it the sermon — he always preached when he visited the churches, and the people always came to hear him.

After the sermon there was added cheer for Dr. Gulick in the musical " *Aloha, Aloha, Aloha* " of this warm-hearted people.

[1] Their pronunciation for Dr. Gulick.

CHAPTER XXII.

POLITICS.

INTENSITY of life was vastly increased after 1864 by the projection of active politics into the life of Hawaii. History tells us that in 1855, at the age of twenty-one, Kamehameha IV became king of the islands; that as a man he was highly educated, brilliant, courteous, and as a king bent on carrying into effect the noble constitution given to his people by Kamehameha III. It also tells us that progress was made while he lived; that he died in 1863; that many hopes were buried with him; and that his elder brother Lot succeeded him as Kamehameha V.

Now the contrasting portraits of these two kings are indicative of their real character, for while the younger brother has a quiet, thoughtful face and eyes that look directly into ours, the elder brother reminds us of a Lot unwaveringly determined to abide in Sodom — a gross neck and heavy features, full cheeks, thick lips, unkindly expression, and eyes which, though looking down, seem to say: "Here I am and you cannot move me."

On the whole, this represents him well, for he

proved to be a strong, resolute, unscrupulous, unyielding man, who, by the power of his single personality, was soon able to overthrow the constitution of 1852 and replace it with another.

Differing from his brother, he believed that the people had too many rights and the king too few. He objected to the liberal constitution of Kamehameha III and resolved to take no oath to maintain it until he had changed it. By proclamation, therefore, on the seventh of May, 1864, he called upon the people for an election of delegates who should meet in Honolulu for the revision and amendment of the constitution.

At once there was surprise and indignation everywhere. This looked like "a step toward absolutism;" yet the king made a tour of the islands in its advocacy, and the election was ordered for the thirteenth of June.

As it happened, the annual meeting of the Evangelical Association, which drew to Honolulu the strongest men from the entire group, was to open on the first of June. Now because in so small a place no department of life could stand in isolation, because, in fact, religious life and political life throbbed with their hearts too close to each other to be easily separated, a significant step was promptly taken by the Hawaiian Board. By special action it postponed the opening of the Evangelical Association from the first to the twenty-seventh of June, and this for the sake of leaving at their posts men who should instruct the people in the dangers involved and guide them in the choice of men.

It was a wise move. Satisfactory men were elected. At twelve o'clock, July 7, 1864, the constitutional convention was opened by the king; it met in the great historic Kawaiahao church. Sixteen nobles and twenty-seven delegates were there, and among them six sons of missionaries. The whole scene was so novel in the annals of Hawaii that history was written that day with an exclamation point. In a building erected by the missionary; guided by intelligence nurtured by the missionary; associated as equals with the sons of the missionary; summoned by a king who owed all his personal education to a missionary, — the Hawaiian people had been called to yield to this king some of the freedom and strength that had come to them through the missionary!

The situation itself is explained by the fact that righteousness had not entered the heart of Kamehameha V and that men from foreign lands who were anti-missionary, anti-Christian, and surprisingly pro-self were the men of whom he sought counsel.

Yet, even among these men, one acknowledged at the time that " the American missionary had brought all the rights the natives ever had." Appreciating this for themselves the people were not ready voluntarily to relinquish these rights; and among others they had sent the sons of their missionaries to wage the constitutional battle for them.

After a week of debate nobles and representatives were seated together as a single voting body, " a great loss for the opposition," said Dr. Gulick, " since in the presence of hereditary chiefs scarce a native can assert anything contrary to their known or supposed wish or thought." Another struggle resulted in the vote that the convention had the right to make a new constitution.

In August, nobles and representatives were still in session. Revision was being attempted; and the intelligence of the Islands was almost breathless as it waited for results. The king's first desire was to limit suffrage by a property qualification. He assured the people that in a monarchy there simply could not be universal suffrage. Native delegates were greatly stirred.

" More than one," says Dr. Gulick, " have this week told his majesty that instead of kindness he is treating his people with unkindness. An Englishman said the other day that 'the American missionaries have certainly taught the natives to think, but that they have learned to think a little too much!'

"Yesterday the matter came to a vote," he continues, "and nearly two thirds of the delegation, most of them natives, in the very face of royalty, calmly stood in the negative while the king with fiery looks counted them one by one. It gives one's blood a new impulse! Immediately the king, instead of having the question of adjournment put as usual, merely dismissed them, bidding them come together on the 13th."

They came, and for five hours again the question was discussed. Again those delegates, in behalf of the very slender purses of their constituents, voted against it, but the king did not yield; a man with that sort of face never does. His action, however, was simple enough; he abrogated the constitution of 1852, prorogued the convention of 1864, and told the nation that in a few days he would proclaim a new constitution! With a thought perhaps of protest from the people, it is recorded that "The police force was at once increased by eighteen men and one man went about with a pistol in his pocket!" A tempest in a teapot, perhaps, but none the less truly a tempest for Hawaii.

On the twentieth of August the new constitution was published. Various natives refused to cheer for it, saying that "it was not for them, but for the chiefs and the foreigners." Dr. Gulick himself felt that "the dial of constitutional liberty has gone back."

Among other changes, this constitution provided for "the imprisonment of any editor or public speaker expressing himself improperly against a law under debate in the House." "Thus is our press muzzled," wrote Dr. Gulick, "and public opinion parried." How little he anticipated the latter personal pressure of this measure upon himself!

Thus did the will of one man overturn the constitution of a nation, and the act had far-reaching results. That was indeed a solemn day for Hawaii: for as a natural outcome of the instability introduced by Kamehameha V, there arose at last so strong a desire for righteous legislation and a constitution beyond the reach of any one man that in 1893 Hawaii deposed her queen, established a provisional government, and seriously offered herself to the United States for annexation.

In November, 1864, the immediate excitement of Hawaiian politics was swept aside for a moment by the thrilling news that Abraham Lincoln had been reëlected President of the United States. Indeed, such enthusiasm and such cheering followed it on Hawaii that "for days afterward some of our best citizens were hoarse." In multiplied numbers the Stars and Stripes floated at once over Honolulu and its harbor, while Americans walked the streets with radiant faces, and Hawaiians as they met each other said: "We feel like Americans to-day."

But all this was only as sunlight piercing a cloud.

The cloud remained for Hawaii and the new era which had now been fairly introduced by Kamehameha V.

At this distance, and to us as to others, the political unrest of those years from 1864 to 1870 is indeed blended now as a picturesque cloud. It overhangs the Islands of Hawaii and serves to heighten the effect of light and shadow resting upon them. And wherefore analyze it to-day? It is enough at this distance to say it was a cloud, that good men shivered under it, that righteousness seemed to stagger, that swayed by the will of royalty, as in other lands, humanity both white and brown did those things that were not expected of them. Through it all, however, good men were unitedly praying for the welfare of Hawaii, and Hawaiians were being educated politically.

"Now I see how it is," said a shrewd anti-missionary observer; "the churches are governed by the membership in a way that is educating the people in democratic principles, and from the church model they have learned how to conduct political affairs."

Those who watched passing events through these years perceived two currents of influence moving across the Hawaiian Islands. On the one hand, in larger numbers than ever before, young men were entering the ministry and turning to the help of their own people; noble missionaries were trying to fit their large mantles to narrower shoulders; churches were multiplying, church membership increasing, and, in proportion to the population, benevolent contributions were growing larger every year. This was the crystal half of that slow-moving *mer de glace*.

The other half was as unsightly as the rock-covered surface of the Taléfre. It had its rise in the corruption that reigned in high places. Intemperance and immorality were making headlong progress. Superstition was revived and its accompanying heathen rites. With a king who towered among his people as a promoter of wrongdoing, it is not strange that for a season spiritual blight rested upon them. Where Kaahumanu and Kapiolani had once stood and pointed the people heavenward, Kamehameha V and his friends now stood and beckoned them downward.

In view of the situation two courses were advocated by those who loved Hawaii. One urged " conciliatory measures," an effort to secure the good of the nation without much show of hostility to the government; an attempt to guide without alienating royal favor lest displeasure bring the greater evil. Certain members of the community even thought "it would be better to follow our Saviour's example, and the example of Paul by keeping aloof from political matters altogether."

The other party, in the front ranks of which Dr. Gulick had now cast himself, claimed that "Christ came not at all times to bring peace, but sometimes the sword," and that "this constant effort to abate strife for the right often works incalculable mischief." It cried: "Our 'lost cause' will yet be won again, and by a force more potent than powder and ball. Stern, steady demand for right, educating the people and daunting wicked rulers are the only means we know." Stern, steady demand was therefore made every week, and its voice to the people was The Kuokoa.[1]

During 1865 The Auokoa had been started as a purely governmental paper. It represented anti-missionary sentiments.

Perhaps it would hardly have been in the natural order of things if The Kuokoa, with its avowed sentiments, had wholly escaped the wrath of the governmental party. In point of fact it did not escape.

It was May, 1866. The Legislature was in session

---

[1] One of the most vital questions at this time was concerning the common schools of the country. Even so early as June, 1866, a startling series of charges against "those who have direction of the schools," the government, was made to the Evangelical Association by its committee on schools. It was asserted that they had appointed as school superintendent with exclusive power over school-teachers, "a man who for a series of years had shown hostility to the Americans"; that "the wishes of parents are utterly disregarded" in the appointment of teachers; that "religious influences" are to be excluded from the schools and the "Bible disallowed"; that Catholic teachers are placed over Protestant schools, "men of immoral character appointed to the office of teacher and trustee," and "schoolhouses sold in districts where there are enough children to sustain a school."

in Honolulu; and in the progress of its business it was moved "that the Assembly order the sergeant-at-arms to bring the person of L. H. Gulick before the House to answer for the publication of a certain article in The Kuokoa of May 12, in which thirteen members of the House by name are called parasites of the Ministers because they voted against the bill to reduce the horse tax from one dollar to fifty cents, stating that these men had no regard for the wishes of the people."

One member was promptly on his feet in favor of the resolution "because The Kuokoa was unanimously respected," he said "and because the people had great confidence in its editor, Dr. Gulick. The people believed The Kuokoa," he added, "and did not believe the government organ, The Auokoa. The Kuokoa's influence was so great that it very nearly prevented elections from being held in certain districts, and therefore this House ought to take notice of the insult." Yet another member did not like to be called a parasite because, though it was false, "the natives in the outer districts would point at him and say: 'There is the member from Honolulu who is *hoopili-meaai*[1] to the Ministers.'"

Other members, however, protested that "the House should be above sensitiveness for such

[1] Parasite.

attacks"; that, if Dr. Gulick were brought before them, "he would have the opportunity of saying he was a victim on the altar of the people."

The motion, nevertheless, was carried, and a warrant was signed and issued "for the production of Dr. Gulick before the House at eleven A.M. to-morrow, or as soon thereafter as possible."

Though it is thirty years since The Kuokoa printed the "communication" which so disturbed the House in 1864, yet its closing words still burn with the fire with which they were written : —

"There, you people of Hawaii, Maui, Molokai, Lanai, Oahu, and Kauai, you can see the faithlessness of your chosen representatives who come here and join hands to that side, leaving you in the hindermost canoe! Look out for the year 1868! It is yours to watch the right!"

Ever its friend, The Commercial Advertiser, now stanchly defended The Kuokoa. It examined Article Fifty-two of the Constitution,[1] and it maintained that there had been no violation of that article; that "the

---

[1] *Article Fifty-two.* — The Legislative Assembly shall have authority to punish by imprisonment not exceeding thirty days, every person not a member who shall be guilty of disrespect to the Assembly, by any disorderly or contemptuous behavior in its presence; or who, during the time of its sitting, shall publish any false report of its proceedings, or insulting comments upon the same: or who shall threaten harm to the body or estate of any of its members for anything said or done in the Assembly, in his way going or returning; or who shall rescue any person arrested by order of the Assembly.

representatives are making themselves ridiculous to the whole people"; that "The Kuokoa might say that the members are a pack of fools and ignoramuses without violating the letter or the spirit of the article." "When, therefore," it continued, "Minister —— says 'the public have a right to comment on the laws, but not on the men who make the laws,' he sets up an issue for which he has no authority to support him. He attempts to erect a bulwark, and getting behind that structure shouts: 'There is no power between us and God!' There is a power between him and God, and he will live to witness it."

These were stern words; but the warrant had been issued, and on the eighteenth of May "the return of the sergeant-at-arms was read, stating that the body of L. H. Gulick was in readiness to be brought before the House."

What a day that was for the family of children in the large white house under the algaroba trees! They only knew that their father had been arrested, and they waited through the hours with a shivering expectancy that something far more dreadful yet was sure to happen. Perhaps they prayed about it, though as yet they were not very pious children. No question, however, as to the praying of their mother; not prayer for deliverance alone, but prayer that wisdom might be given to her husband.

He was brought before the Assembly and replied laconically to the questions of the Vice-President.

"Are you editor and publisher of the newspaper Kuokoa, published in Honolulu?"

"I am."

"Do you hold yourself responsible for articles published in it?"

"I do."

Then he was remanded and the members discussed his case. There was much excitement.

"I was the member," said one, "who moved that this person be brought before this House, and I now move that he be punished according to Article Fifty-two of the Constitution."

Two or three others were on their feet at once. One asked for the law that could punish a man for saying certain representatives were parasites. He moved that the resolution be tabled and Dr. Gulick set free. Others supported this. Yet another moved that the manuscript of the article be brought into the House. Still another said: "Having in mind the dignity of this people, I demand that this person be punished, else he may go away and do worse." Another desired authority first, precedent. "I don't think a person from Hawaii to Niihau," he said, "was ever punished for calling another *hoopilimeaai*."

In the midst of these differing expressions of

opinion a line was brought in from Dr. Gulick himself : —

To His Highness, M. Kekuanaoa, *President of the Legislative Assembly.*

Sir, — Before the Assembly pass to any resolution of condemnation in my case, allow me to crave the common right of a criminal of speaking in my own defense.   Yours respectfully,
L. H. Gulick.

This was not allowed, however, and after further discussion a motion was made and seconded, amended, amended again, and passed, that —

"The Rev. L. H. Gulick be brought again before the bar and be admonished that this House do consider the article a contempt to this Assembly, and with this intimation to him we do dismiss the further consideration of his case."

Promptly, therefore, he was "brought again," and the President said : —

" I do hereby inform you that you have committed a contempt of this Assembly, and would say, Do so no more ; and with this say to you, Go from this House."

So he went quietly away; but the old flash was in his eye and his love for Hawaii had grown stronger and not weaker through this trial for her. "I feel so indifferent as to anything but duty," he wrote, "that I think it alone gives me vantage ground."

CHAPTER XXIII.

TANGLED THREADS.

KEENLY sensitive as he was to adverse criticism, Dr. Gulick remained nevertheless uninfluenced by it. His hand still guided The Kuokoa. Though the friction of it often bruised him, still he neither flinched nor left half undone what duty seemed to him to require. And this because, as he said, "We have fallen on times when there is need of manhood, when cringing and weakness only defeat our cause."

"To one thing I am pledged," he adds, " and that is not to err on the side of extreme lukewarmness to the interests of the Hawaiian race. I know the danger, and I propose being careful; but I am a man, and I am an American, and I desire that America's influence should be more directly felt for the good of the monarchy and for the people's sake and for the cause of evangelical religion."

Thus was he an American; but he was so joined to both countries that it is somewhat difficult to tell which was dearer to him. In truth, he belonged to both, for on another page he says: "We beg you to remember that we younger men are not foreign missionaries, but to all practical purposes native Hawaiians, only claiming for our darker-skinned fellow citizens what has been ruthlessly filched from them by the help of foreign talent and foreign wickedness."

Because of this double allegiance Dr. Gulick welcomed the annexation discussions of 1868. He saw at once the faintly outlined answer to various Hawaiian problems and dared thus to prophesy: —

"The time will come when we shall be ready for absorption by the Great Republic if they desire it. At present we are not ready, but these discussions are preparing the way." And further: "Be assured that the time will come when manhood, suffrage, and a truly representative government will be secured for Hawaii."

In doing what he could to hasten this time, Dr. Gulick walked constantly and swiftly under a very heavy load. For, in addition to his duties as Corresponding Secretary and his personal charge of the whole publication department of the mission,[1] he carried for years "the entire editorship and pecuniary responsibility of the newspaper Kuokoa. I do not at all regret having thus far done the work," he writes, "but it is too much for one man."

[1] "Which includes the supervision of the press and the charge of the distribution and sale of the publications, and the keeping of all the book and newspaper accounts with our ministry throughout the group."

This we realize. Yet there was still the added weight of frequent pulpit supply for the unusually intelligent foreign audience of Fourth Street Church; Fourth of July and other orations for the same foreign audience, and once that thrilling memorial address, still remembered, when Hawaii no less than America mourned the tragic death of Abraham Lincoln.

Surely those were busy years; but the upper and nether millstones of political life and church life never spared him; and we are not surprised that his " spirits sometimes sank," that he " longs sometimes to be out of these complications, to go to Micronesia or Marquesas." But this was only the discouragement of a moment.

Encouragement came in the line of immediate church work. Annual reports mark the steps of its progress; and a note with a touch of humor in it shows the large coöperation of those who were working together for Hawaii: —

"The native ministry is stepping on even faster than we radicals had expected, and our conservative fathers are pushing the wheels where even we shrink. The world moves somewhat, even if a little one-sidedly. We will rejoice."

No question as to cause for rejoicing, for the summarized results of this coöperation showed in 1869 fifty-six organized churches, thirty-six ordained Hawaiian pastors and eight licentiates; thirteen Hawaiian foreign missionaries; a church membership of twelve thousand four hundred and ninety-seven, and benevolent contributions of $29,386 for that year alone.[1]

Where, in 1863, but four churches had Hawaiian pastors, the case was now reversed. In 1869 "but four missionaries of the American Board had pastoral charge of the Hawaiian Islands — all on the island of Hawaii."

As part of the work of the Hawaiian Board, larger provision had been desired for the education of Hawaiian girls. Miss Ogden still carried on her school at Makiki. In 1865 Mr. and Mrs. Orramel Gulick moved to Waialua their girls' school started on Hawaii. This grew rapidly. But Honolulu was

[1] This seems small as compared to the larger numbers of earlier years. But the fact should be borne in mind that the race itself was passing rapidly away. A Hawaiian population estimated by the first missionaries to be 130,000 had dwindled to 84,000 in 1850. The excess of deaths over births during the same years 2,890. Through 1867, 1868, and 1869 the average annual decrease was 1,154. Indeed, the population of the Islands diminished so rapidly that by 1872 it numbered but 56,800. Concerning this fact Dr. Gulick wrote at the time:—

"But for the conserving effects of the gospel during the last half century, there would have been now scarce a Hawaiian left to tell the story of the extinction of the race through foreign vices grafted upon native depravity. That the race still continues to decrease is no wonder, but that it is in existence to-day, with any manifestations of true Christianity, is one of the modern miracles of grace. That there is so much vice and immorality should astonish no one, but that there is any virtue, any piety, any civilization should cause us to shout over the triumphs of redeeming mercy."

in need. Dr. Gulick was already overworked, and his wife was not very strong. She had five young children of her own and had welcomed as her own the children sent to Honolulu by her "missionary sisters" in Micronesia, yet Mrs. Gulick felt that her opportunity had come. No one else could begin the school. She had been "longing for more missionary work to do, praying for open doors." On the sixth of March, 1865, we find the sequel to her prayer:—

"Opened school this morning with eight scholars. Our cook is sick, Mrs. B. still in bed, and our friends from Micronesia are here. We are twenty-one in the family."

That day school of eight was Kawaiahao Seminary in its infancy. Through succeeding months numbers increased, boarders were accepted, neighbors helped Mrs. Gulick in the teaching, until at last the need of permanent help was imperative. Miss Lydia Bingham was then called to the work and reached it in 1867.

In the meantime, however, Kawaiahao Seminary remained in every sense a family school, which studied and played and created much confusion and needed much employment; all of it to be devised and the machinery of it to be kept in motion by the one busy brain of the mother of them all — the precious, prayerful woman whose life was so full of active kindnesses to others that her children never heard her gossip or say unkind things about her neighbors.

There were so many children in this family school, and they did things so in flocks, that names are seldom mentioned. We simply know from Mrs. Gulick's journal that "most of our sixteen children have had colds," that "on Sunday six were sick," that "on Saturday I went with nine children to the woods"; that on another Saturday "we had carriages to take nineteen of us and horses for three more"; that "five rode while fifteen walked to church"; that "we all went out to Manoa to bathe."

Instead of groaning in spirit under the turmoil of such a life Mrs. Gulick is exultant. "Oh, how wonderful," she exclaims, "is the goodness of God and his minute care over his children!"

Though the central abiding place of this family was the home in Honolulu where the Kawaiahao Seminary still stands, yet in charming Manoa valley there was a small painted cottage bought with money earned by Mrs. Gulick in teaching before she was married. Hither they hied for their holidays and their vacation times. Such a paradise it seemed to them all! Sweet jasmine and roses, and vines in profusion, and guava trees and pasture lands, and a short exciting cut across lots over the stone walls to that spot of all enchantment — their bathing place in the beautiful stream!

Here too Dr. Gulick often went with them, and there is a tradition that he lay awake one night planning the location of garden spots for his own and the other children to cultivate. More likely, however, he lay awake under his own increasing weariness and perplexity. Gradually he had realized that there were those who felt that, as Secretary of the Hawaiian Board, he should be less pronounced in his politics, less radical in his demands, more conservative, more silent; that, with skirts drawn judiciously aside from political touch and with quiet upturned face and finger pointing heavenward, he should make no very audible protest, though his countrymen were being charmed and chained and dragged past him to their destruction; that, in other words, he should attend to what seemed to them more legitimately the affairs of the heavenly kingdom, leaving earthly politics to those not so officially situated.

But it is certain that Dr. Gulick had no moment of doubt as to his own duty in the matter. "I make in my mind a very important distinction," he says, "between the proper neutral political position of a foreign missionary and one like myself to the 'manor born.' I should as soon think of changing my course as of being silent regarding theft or murder."

No one ever questioned Dr. Gulick's loyalty to Hawaii, his courage or his ability. Those who differed from him, the conservatives and a few of the older missionaries, did certainly assert that he was "too radical"; but they also testified to his "executive ability," to his "faithfulness" and "effectiveness as a worker."

Since his own conviction remained unchanged, however, and since there also existed this other expressed conviction as to the political duties of a Secretary, Dr. Gulick saw with increasing distinctness that his next great step must accomplish for him a withdrawal from his position as Secretary of the Hawaiian Board: for he could not consent to be a divisive element in it. The thought dawned slowly but fully upon him.

"I am willing to leave my office and my country for my country's good and to disembarrass the cause of Christ," he wrote, "but I cannot recede from my position of antagonism to what I consider wrong."

"Thanks for your kindly exhortation to keep up a 'brave heart.' It is just what I intend to do, the Lord helping me, even if necessary to the point of standing one side as soon as it shall appear that my portion of the work is done; and it requires more nerve, I fancy, to do this than to cling to office under the impression that my services in this particular sphere are indispensable to the Lord!"

The decision was seriously made, and on the twenty-seventh of January, 1870, by letter to the Hawaiian

Board, Dr. Gulick asked for three months' leave of absence and declined reëlection as its Secretary.

Of necessity there was protest. Even those who differed from him in politics were anxious to retain his help for mission work. They wrote to the Secretaries in Boston about it and said: —

"There is probably not one of the missionaries who will not cordially and earnestly sustain Dr. Gulick, nor one who has not done so in his proper work as a Secretary of the Mission Board. He has had and still has the coöperation of his brethren in his missionary labors in an unusual degree. He is a good and diligent officer, prompt in business and devoted to the cause. I hope you may persuade Dr. Gulick and his brother[1] to listen to the voice of their brethren in continuing their missionary work, even though they may not be sustained in political matters or any other outside of what some of us esteem to be their proper sphere of labor."

Then too there were tender words of appreciation from his friends.

"Your years of faithful service here," one of them wrote, "have been productive of greater and far more important results than you certainly can estimate — or I either. Our entire work has been modified by the agency to which, under God, you have been called —

[1] Rev. O. H. Gulick was leaving Hawaii at the same time.

savingly modified ; nor will the impress you have been privileged to put upon it ever be lost."

"Personally, dear brother," he continues, "I should not like to trust myself to tell you how these years of earnest toil and precious companionship with you in the Master's work here loom up in the history of my life, as above all other portions thereof — years of warm-hearted, constant, effective work under God for this poor people. And now all around me, go where I may, my thoughts find you, and my heart as well as my mind perceives your tracks ineffaceable on all departments of our work. God honored you much, though in a comparatively obscure sphere, to do a great service for him."

In spite of protest and appreciation, however, the path of duty seemed very clear to Dr. Gulick, and his work for Hawaii ended in February, 1870.

For a minute account of all he attempted and all he succeeded in doing for the land of his birth one must turn to the multitudes of letters and reports which were written at the time. Some of these are gathered in Honolulu, while several hundred other letters have found their way to the American Board Department of the Congregational Library in Boston.

The signatures of these letters are as signboards along the course of Dr. Gulick's life on Hawaii: —

"For the cause of evangelical religion yours."

"Yours for right and freedom and the triumph of Christ's kingdom." "Yours hopefully." "Yours in Christian bonds." "Yours in solicitude and hope." "Yours in sadness." "Yours in perplexity." "Yours in the furnace."

But the last letter had been written. He had parted again from wife and children and aged parents; and now, in the gloaming, he stood alone behind the pilot house and once more watched with dimmed eye the fading outline of the land he passionately loved. He was returning to Boston to talk about the future missionary course of his life. And while his heart ached, he could not anticipate the earnest voice that should, years after, try to call him home again; nor realize that his life on Hawaii had prepared him to enter a wider door and a larger work in other lands.

CHAPTER XXIV.

PAPAL LANDS.

FROM what had sometimes seemed the furnace there was abrupt change of atmosphere when Dr. Gulick found himself quietly seated in the cordial serenity of the Mission Rooms in Boston. Indeed, the sort of intensity which gave peculiar interest to his Hawaiian experiences was never repeated for him. Necessarily, therefore, the year 1870 marked a turning point in his life. The subsequent steps in its course were, however, in harmony with the strength of character which life in Micronesia and Hawaii had already demonstrated. For years these steps forced their way through strangely new and varied scenes.

Though early appointed by the Prudential Committee to act as district secretary for New England, the arrangement was temporary. And this because, as he says: "I pressed so hard to go abroad again, even to Micronesia if there were no other door open, that I am still to be considered a foreign missionary at home to get ready for another stage of labor. Indeed, the idea is quite distinct that we go to Micronesia by and by if Providence favors."

Until the last of 1871 he therefore acted as district secretary, "flying about like a shuttlecock," he says, "on the Master's business, as I suppose."

During this time his family joined him. During this time also it came to pass that "five brothers of us were together for about fifteen minutes." A notable event in a family whose living members had never yet been all together at any time.

Charles Finney Gulick had died during his student life in America; and of the remaining six brothers three [1] were already engaged in foreign missionary work, while two others [2] were soon to enter upon it. Later yet the sixth brother [3] and the sister [4] joined the same service.

In their devotion to duty, though it led to this world-wide sort of separation, the need of a new kind of courage came suddenly to Dr. and Mrs. Gulick. While still in Hawaii they had lent their youngest son to their bereaved brother Orramel and his wife, who petitioned for him; a loan of a few weeks at first, but one that was lengthened into months.

Both families had come to America. The brother and his wife were assigned to Japan. And because

---

[1] Orramel Hinckley, soon to sail for Japan, John Thomas in China, and Luther Halsey.

[2] William Hooker, who accompanied his brother Halsey to Spain, and Thomas Lafon, who joined them a year later.

[3] Theodore Weld.

[4] Julia Ann Eliza.

"the Prudential Committee did not advise my going to Micronesia," writes Dr. Gulick, "and because I wished to remain either in or on the Pacific Ocean, at my own request I go to Japan too, and with the cordial approval of the committee."

The two families were to be together. And since, under this arrangement, the child would still feel the nearness of his mother and share the companionship of his brothers, with characteristic unselfishness he was lent again to the home which was desolate without him.

Mr. and Mrs. Orramel Gulick preceded the others to Japan, and the little boy of three went with them. His parents were to follow soon. Weeks passed. Their boxes had been shipped to San Francisco. Final preparations had all been made, and the next steamer that sailed was to take them to Japan. At this point there was a sudden reversal of decision. The American Board accepted a call to work in Roman Catholic countries, and wished to have the experience of Dr. Gulick in the establishment of its work in Spain.

"It is hard," says Mrs. Gulick, "to refuse to listen to the combined wisdom of such honored men as the secretaries of the Board and Dr. Anderson, so we have consented to go. The severe trial is that in not going to Japan we cannot join our precious little one there. Indeed, the thought of not being able soon to see my darling child is very hard to bear. Yet we do it for Christ, and willingly, as so much less than he has done for us." It was well perhaps that the brave mother could not know just then that she should never see her little son on earth again.

"I acquiesce," writes the father, "though my heart is in the Pacific Ocean."

In the mean time the friends who had already reached Japan were preparing to welcome them.

"Ollie[1] plans everything now with reference to Luther's[2] coming," writes Mrs. Orramel Gulick; "has a bamboo gun and other things all ready for him. He thinks his crib is not large enough for both himself and Luther to sleep in, and yesterday morning prayed that God would teach us how to make the crib larger when Luther comes. Only two weeks from to-morrow the steamer will be here!"

When it reached them, instead of the friends whom they expected, and for Ollie, his small brother, there were letters which told them that those dear ones were not coming at all: that they were going to Spain instead.

Thus it came about that twenty years after they first left Boston for Micronesia, and with heroism as real now as that which moved them then, Dr. and

---

[1] Orramel, named for his uncle.
[2] His next older brother.

Mrs. Gulick set out again from the same port in an opposite direction.

Soon after that it was Spain, but Spain without her fabled "castles." Far more real, indeed, was the poverty which appalled them as they met it in public places, and the pitiful begging for "charity, madam, for the love of God." "Such pinched and wan faces that followed us everywhere," writes Mrs. Gulick. "Such rags and tatters that fluttered in the breeze, and told of such suffering and such want!" Such old, old civilization and poverty handed down for so many generations! All this was to be seen while the memory was still fresh of well-oiled, well-fed, physically comfortable Micronesia.

And now, though Europe was both historically and geographically separated from the heathen world, yet living there did by no means indicate a separation from other mission fields. China, Japan, Micronesia, Hawaii, America, and Spain were linked together by the letters which each member of the family wrote and received, and which, by prearrangement, each forwarded to the next in order. This signified large drafts on slender purses, for, says Dr. Gulick, "I paid about fifty dollars postage on private matter during six months in 1872."[1] Yet it was an invest-

---

[1] In this connection he begged that family letters should be folded with the first page outward, claiming that "this rule followed would save about a month's time in the Gulick family per year."

ment with a purpose. Because of it a family otherwise divided by oceans and by continents stood as a unit in its purposes and convictions. And so far as intimacy with mission fields was concerned this correspondence secured for the brothers not simply a broadened outlook, but the practical removal of horizon limits.

Spain offered much to write about, for her towering history and its monuments ranged themselves as a gorgeous background to her faded present life.

"Yesterday I visited ancient Saguntum," writes Dr. Gulick, "founded (so Murray says, and Murray knows!) 1384 years before Christ. I am vexed with myself for having gaped so often over paltry places and objects five hundred and one thousand years old! I sat me down on the steps of the Roman amphitheater, saw the inscription of P. Scipio two hundred years before Christ, saw the gate called Hannibal's, and at last I began to have a realizing sense that there may have been such people as Greeks, Romans, Carthaginians, and such individuals as Scipio, Hannibal, and the Cæsars."

After all, however, the present was even more real to him than this vivid past. And being settled in their home in Barcelona, while he studied the language he also taught in the small girls' school which they opened at once, arranged for the permanent establishment of their work at different points in northern Spain, and did much toward the advancement of unity among the Christians of Barcelona. He furthermore studied the foreign workers throughout the country, their theories, their methods, and the practical outcome of the combination of the two. Results followed. He soon stood as a general on an eminence. His eye ranged the whole field.

Contrasts were necessarily drawn between all that pertained to humanity in Europe and in the Pacific. This did not always place Europe in the light: neither did it always shadow the Pacific. It appeared, indeed, that in methods of work and in types of Christian character developed, Spain herself often suffered by the contrast. The cloud which cast this shadow upon her in 1872 was the apparent lack of all attempt to develop self-supporting churches. It was a contrast to the zeal with which Christians worked for themselves and others in the Pacific. England, Germany, and France had each sent missionaries to Spain; but their policy was not of the self-supporting type which is held as the ideal in the missions of the American Board. On the contrary, Dr. Gulick found that almost everything was done for the Spanish converts.

"Foreign money builds or hires the churches," he says, "pays the sexton, buys the melodeon, pays the whole of the salaries of the native preachers and teachers, and, in fact, does everything for them but their eating and their sleeping. They are in consequence about ruined for Christian work. To become a Protestant is to be saved by grace and emancipated from all work. The idea of Protestantism is, indeed, so strongly that of 'free grace' here that the fact of its requiring 'good works' is forgotten, and we shall have hard work in teaching it."

On the other hand, there were cheering conditions even in 1872: "From three to four thousand who profess to be evangelical Christians, over twenty-five reported church organizations, and two thousand children under evangelical instruction daily."

Of necessity these figures involved the vital question as to the true missionary position to take toward Spanish Christians and their churches. Meeting this query, Dr. Gulick recommended that "the foreign missionary clearly apprehend the distinction between missionary and ecclesiastical questions," and that, while retaining "unflinching control of the former," he should "avoid more than an advisory position toward ecclesiastical matters. If the missionary tries by voting to control the action of the native churches, they will, by voting, attempt to control his missionary action."

Two and a half years were spent in this work of

beginnings.[1] The mission to Spain was fairly on its feet, and the Prudential Committee now asked Dr. Gulick to join its work in Italy.

"Just the man we want for that field," writes the Secretary, Dr. Clark, "to take special oversight of our developed work, to bring the young churches into line. You will of course go to Florence: that is our Italian headquarters."[2]

"From Micronesia to Italy!" exclaims Dr. Gulick. "Could contrasts be greater? From the negation of all Art to the very mother of all the fine arts! From the center of the Pacific to the center of Europe!"

And then in August, 1873: "In Italy! It seems like romance! I can hardly realize it."

Though it looked as if all previous experience had been but preparation for this new work; and though Dr. and Mrs. Gulick greatly desired to be rid of packing, and moving, and house hunting, and to find for themselves a permanent home at last; and though no land could have been more charming and no friends more cordial than those whom they found in Italy, yet, as it happened, the stay there was not for many months. It ended because of their honest adherence

---

[1] Rev. William H. Gulick was located at Santander, since removed to San Sebastian, and Rev. Thomas L. Gulick spent seven years of his nine years in Spain, in Zaragoza.

[2] Rev. Mr. Alexander was already a missionary of the American Board in Italy. "He will devote himself specially," wrote Dr. Clark, "to the training school we desire to start."

to conviction regardless of personal sacrifice. Summarized, the following was the situation: —

The work of the American Board was in conjunction with the Free Church of Italy.[1] Unfortunately, to a certain extent, the same defects characterized work in Italy as in Spain. And in Dr. Gulick's thought two of these were most prominent: —

First: the indefiniteness of the idea that "the church must consist only of those who hope they have undergone a change of heart and give evidence of it."

Second: the lack of organization, "with special reference to assuming all possible responsibility specially regarding their own work." For example, "the Free Church has had," he continues, "a year of unusual prosperity: that is, they have had very large receipts of money from England and America, and have, consequently, done less for themselves than they did last year."

As weeks passed, he was increasingly convinced, as he says, that "the work of the Board in Italy will be the most unsatisfactory of all their missions and the most expensive." And also that "there will not be

---

[1] In this organization, thirty-five churches were "associated under a rather indefinite church government which savored partly of Congregationalism and partly of Presbyterianism." Ten of these churches were placed under the care of the American Board. And judging the Free Church by a meeting of its Assembly in Pisa, Dr. Gulick early pronounced many of "their ideas of business definite and on the whole good though different somewhat from the Anglo-American style."

any great success in their work here on any true basis for indefinite years to come."

At this point the American Board experienced serious financial embarrassment. Curtailment was necessary somewhere; and Dr. Gulick's judgment indicated that the place for it was in Italy.

"But I need hardly tell you," he writes to Dr. Clark, "that it requires some nerve on my part to give you thus fully what I conceive to be the unhopeful side of things." And later: —

"I am increasingly doubtful of the wisdom of holding on in Italy. But I cannot tell you how much I dread another removal."

It ended as he felt was best. The decision was made, and the withdrawal of the Board from Italy took place "because our financial necessities compel us to retrenchment."

There was rapid movement of events for Dr. Gulick through the closing four months of 1874. A visit to Turkey was permitted. And Greece with its history and its classic suggestions lay on his course. What a contrast to Micronesia with no history! As he sailed, he was "reminded of Homer and of the exploits of Ulysses." He passed Actium, saw "the mountains of Peloponnesus dim in the east;" realized that "not far to the southeast, though it could not be seen, was ancient Olympia;" crossed the Gulf of

Messina; touched at Cerijo and wished it had not been smoky that he "might have seen Crete, where Paul was wrecked." After Milo, and Paros, and Syra, with "Delos the sacred" in the distance, they reached Athens.

"I might have whizzed up in ten minutes on the railroad," he says, "but thought it more respectful to the shades of Demosthenes, Socrates, Plato, and Aristotle to ride in the light of a full moon, in a carriage that offered itself. An unexpected flash of sentimentality," he adds, "and my financial necessities were more nearly reconciled than usual!"

Yet no delight in the wonders of the place served to draw him from his purpose to study Christian workers everywhere and their methods of working. This occupied more time in Athens than his sight-seeing. In Constantinople it was the same.[1] While constantly there was inspiration for him in "crossing and recrossing the track of St. Paul and all the ancient gods."

At last, however, with his friend Mr. Bliss for a companion; with worldly possessions of cot-beds "on which to sleep out of the reach of bugs, fleas, rats, etc.," with a tea-pot, a tea-kettle, a coffee-pot, a skillet, a spirit-lamp, knives and forks, spoons, plates, cups, all of tin; with various sorts of food to nourish

---

[1] "As yet I have done almost no sight-seeing, but I am laying up grand stores of missionary knowledge. I am wonderfully favored."

them and huge leathern bags to carry all this property, he started on his journey of eleven hundred miles through Central Turkey. A servant accompanied them on one horse, the goods went upon another, and each traveler had his patient little beast to carry him. Thus the small caravan visited the eastern churches and was warmly welcomed everywhere. In truth it seemed to Dr. Gulick as if " the missionary families rivaled each other in doing all they could for us."

He of the newest visited these of the oldest of the missions of the American Board. And wherever he went he was urged to tell them of his Micronesian and Hawaiian life. An interpreter was always needed; and once, at a very small town, two were required because there was no one there who understood both Arabic and English.

" My words were, therefore, first interpreted into Armenian," he says, " and then into Arabic. It was rather interesting for me to fire off my gun, then wait for the fire to run along Mr. Bliss and Shimas before I could see the result. There was a long interval between the flash and the final report!"

After one of these talks one day, there came to see him an Armenian woman whose thrilling life story told of conversion, persecution, and faithfulness. It furthermore appeared that, years before, she had made a contribution of her golden ornaments toward the building of the Morning Star. For this reason, it was not strange, perhaps, that when the visit was over neither Dr. Gulick nor the Turkish lady felt that Turkey and Micronesia were very far apart.

The travelers had spent thirty-five days on horseback, had journeyed eleven hundred miles, and had visited Constantinople, Thessalonica, Samakov, Samsoon, Marsovan, Cæsarea, Sivas, Harpoot, Diarbekr, Mardin, Urfa, Aintab, Marash, and many smaller towns. They had also crossed the Tigris and Euphrates. "Thoughts have crowded wonderfully," writes Dr. Gulick, "as I have looked on at least a part of the land where Abraham lived, and from whence he started for the promised land of Canaan."

After that it was Europe again, and Italy with the question of future location still to be decided.

The mission to Austria begged for him there. He therefore visited them and submitted the question to the Prudential Committee. They felt, however, that the need of help was greater just then in Boston than in Austria, and sent the decision to him by a cable dispatch. Yielding to their wish, Dr. Gulick turned at once toward America.

CHAPTER XXV.

TO THE PACIFIC AGAIN.

DR. GULICK had taken steamer to cross the Atlantic.[1] "My last act," he says, "was to go to Westminster and drop my tears — literally — on Livingstone's tomb — the noblest shrine in England." The work to which Dr. Gulick was primarily called in Boston was that of raising money for nominally Christian lands. In addition to this, however, and because of Dr. Clark's illness, he was temporarily pressed into the duties of the Foreign Secretary and the consultations of the Prudential Committee.

In July, 1875, he was "taxed to the utmost and taking medicines constantly." He was preparing for the Annual Meeting of the American Board. "I am specially busy these days," he says, "writing up the annual reports of various missions. Have finished those of Papal Lands, and am engaged on that of Japan and Micronesia. Next week I take hold of the Turkish missions." In August he was tired, indeed, but "about through with the entire foreign part of the Annual Report."

---
[1] His family joined him six months later.

While he worked thus intimately at the headquarters in Boston, various methods pleased him, and various other methods did not please him in the line of home policy. Very little can be said here on either side. Very little ought to be said in the line of criticism; for, in his personal relations, nothing could have been kinder or more appreciative than the constant attitude of the Board toward himself and toward his judgment of mission affairs. In fact, so far as investigation of manuscript proves any point, we learn that of his many suggestions made to the Board through his twenty-five years' connection with it, all but one were followed.[1]

Much as he enjoyed the work which he did in Boston and in New England, the current of his life seemed broken in upon. He was doing that which others, he felt, could do as well as he, and for which they might easily be secured. The foreign field seemed still to call him. Then, too, there was with him an instinct for maintaining, at whatever cost, the continuity of his life. Or, as he expressed it: —

"My fixed determination has always been to work abroad, in one land if not in another, rather than give up altogether. So now, while there are reasons for my giving up my lifelong course, and while to many

---

[1] This was in their appointment of a man, whom he sincerely believed to be unworthy, to the position as Trustee of Oahu College.

my determination to go to foreign fields again may seem strange, yet my own understanding of the case is that it comes from a wish to preserve the unity of my life. With characteristic self-abnegation my wife has encouraged my going even without her.[1] And there is another thought which tends to keep me abroad as long as possible, the hope that it will make the foreign work more attractive to my children than it might otherwise be. It will be a proud and happy day when I can welcome them to mission service. I hope and pray that I may be permitted to hold on till then!"

This was his desire. And though at forty-seven he was too old to begin a new language, and though Micronesia was still inexpedient for him, and though for these reasons he could not very well go out as a foreign missionary in connection with the American Board, another way was, nevertheless, opened to him. He received a call from the American Bible Society. In their behalf, China and Japan were offered to him as a field.[2]

This stood on one hand to choose if he wished, while, on the other, was a position with the American Board as "District Secretary for South New England,

---

[1] It was necessary for Mrs. Gulick to remain in the country for the sake of the children.

[2] In their work it was not necessary for him to have intimate knowledge of the languages of the two countries.

with center in Boston and seat in the Prudential Committee." It did not take him many hours to make the choice. And the officers of the Board could only bid him Godspeed; for they loved the heathen world only as much less than he as their sacrifices for it had been less than his.

" Japan, after all ! " he exclaims again.

This time it was Japan in very truth, the Japan which all the world knows so much about to-day, but which, in 1876, was full of its mysteries and its interests, its queer Oriental civilization with all that was charming about it, and its new civilization of the West which was unfolding itself before the bright, almond eyes of the astonished people.

Mrs. Gulick, with three sons and a daughter, had remained in California. A fourth son had already been welcomed to the home of Dr. and Mrs. S. P. Leeds in Hanover, New Hampshire, while a second daughter accompanied her father to Japan.

The City of Pekin, with its roominess and its luxury, was a pleasanter place for worldly comfort than the Morning Star had been when father and daughter first sailed together upon this same Pacific. Yet the splendid steamer lacked the halo of the children's prayers !

After twenty days of sailing, they landed at Yokohama, telegraphed the news to Rev. Orramel H.

Gulick, in Kobé, and received by return message the crushing news that the precious child whom they all loved had died two days before. Gone back to God before the mother, whose heart still ached for her little son, had had a chance to see him and hold him in her arms again! The blow seemed almost cruel. But in the thought of the mother herself, no cruelty ever comes to his children from their heavenly Father. To her it was only a mystery, and through the tightened pain about her heart she simply drew nearer to God and thanked him for the confidence with which she still could trust him.

CHAPTER XXVI.

ADJUSTMENT.

THOUGH Dr. Gulick never regretted the step which carried him from the American Board to the American Bible Society; though, on the contrary, the same situation repeated would have resulted always in the same decision of adherence to foreign missionary work, still, with so strong a nature as his, pain necessarily accompanied this transfer of intimate relations from one great missionary body to another. He calls it "the wrench of his life," his "divorcement."

This was not strange, for his heart and his life were part of the living tissue of the American Board. Her arms had been about him in his cradle; he had lisped childish petitions for her welfare when he first began to pray; the strength of his manhood had been spent in her service; while her officers were his friends and her missionaries his kin. For twenty-five years he had spoken to them through The Missionary Herald, and now to be silent there; to belong suddenly to another organization and to another kind of work; to reach his world through other channels, — all this combined to make a cross which grew heavier for months as he carried it.

This proved to be a transitional period of his life, and the pain which marked it was the more intense because he was nervously exhausted when the need of the adjustment came to him.

"I have no doubt the divine plan is being and will be worked out regarding me," he writes; "but it will not be without suffering on my part, which is inevitable."

"You little know the sense of loneliness which often comes and remains over me. All my missionary connections are broken. There is no mission that claims me as its own. I am a stranger even to the missions of the American Board."

"A sense of isolation surges in upon me and threatens to drown every other emotion. I begin to feel that I am hereafter to look back rather than forward. Yet such a life of breaks is hard to gather up; hard to collect into a useful whole. I don't like the retrospect particularly, and yet from step to step I have tried to do the best."

"My spirits are depressed. It is a dense, suffocating cloud resting down upon me which I have simply got to endure till it lifts. The only way I know is to shut one's lips and let the nervous system twang itself into silence."

For months this sense of loneliness was the saddened undercurrent of his life. It was the harder to bear because Mrs. Gulick was detained in California a year by the needs of their children, and because in the mean time his days were necessarily spent in traveling alone and in making new acquaintances. The truth is that traveling, for its own sake, had lost its fascination for him.

"I am loth to strike out again into the cold ocean of traveling and isolation," he says; "but I will nerve myself up, hold my breath, and plunge in. I shall get through somehow, and then it will not seem so dreadful."

"I don't quite see how it is," he writes at another time, "that one so dependent on family life and love is so tossed away from it. Though my exterior does not betray the fact, I believe I am more dependent on a wife than most men. We Gulicks are as cold as ice outside; as hot as fire within."

"It has been hard enough in the past — much harder than anybody has known — to tear myself away from wife and children; so hard this time that it seemed as though I should succumb under it."

"I long for you so that I sometimes feel as if I could not endure it."

But having set his teeth together and nerved himself to meet it, he stepped through this inevitable pain and loneliness into happiness and work which was increasingly full of satisfaction to him. With it there was the exhilaration which comes when every faculty is strained to the utmost. His personal experience, his grasp of practical methods, his power as an organizer, his acquaintance with the missionary work of the world were all joined for his success.

Furthermore, in the rush of pressing duties his thoughts were carried more and more constantly away from himself. Enthusiasm was aroused and full contentment was coming to him.

His wife and younger children joined him in 1877. While he waited for them he had himself been rather amused at the volume of his writing.

"I don't believe that husband ever wrote to wife much more faithfully," he says, "by day and by night, abroad and at home, when busy and when at leisure, when wakeful and when sleepy, when receiving letters and when receiving none!" But at last she was coming, and he writes: —

"I tremble as I hope and plan. It seems as if I could not wait six days to see you. My heart never yearned so toward absent loved ones as at the present moment. God keep you safely! Words are tame!"

Thus he waited as eagerly for his family among the millions of Japan as he had waited once before quite alone on Ponape. And when they arrived in safety the final, and on the whole the most joyful, era of his life was fairly entered upon.

"I find my work very congenial," he says, "and I have been received with kindness by the American missionaries of all denominations. Already large responsibilities are on my hands."

CHAPTER XXVII.

THE AGED PARENTS.

NO sketch of Dr. Gulick's life would be complete without referring to the closing years of the lives of his parents. They were seventy-six and seventy-seven years old respectively when they left Hawaii for Japan. The reason for the move was the fact that they were growing feeble; that in fulfillment of their prayers their six sons were engaged in foreign missionary work, while their daughter was also summoned to it, and that rather than permit any child to leave his work for the sake of caring for them in their old age, they preferred to go to their children instead. It therefore came to pass that their son Orramel had gone to Hawaii to take his parents and his sister back to Kobé with him.

Almost half a century had passed since Grandfather Gulick, as he was affectionately called, had even seen the outline of his native land. From the energy and ambition of young manhood, the years had changed him into an old man. His shoulders were bent now, and his hair was white. But his thin, keen face and his eyes, still as blue as the sky, beamed with pleasure at the sight of San Francisco. In truth, Rip Van Winkle himself did not return to greater changes, for steam and electricity had acted the part of magicians since he left the world almost fifty years before. And now, for the first time in his life, the venerable man rode upon a railroad train and sent his thoughts over telegraph wires.

From San Francisco they went to Japan. And thereafter, until the aged saints went to heaven, the Kobé home seemed a gateway to Beulah Land.

Grandfather Gulick himself was the first to pass through it. And in his private memorandum book there are foreshadowings of the change. On the twelfth of March, 1877, he reached the pinnacle of his eighty years, and his entry made that day is a characteristic retrospect.

"The close of this day," he writes, "will complete my fourscore years in this world — twenty-nine thousand two hundred and twenty days. Solemn thought! And how little have I done for Him who created me, died to redeem me, and has preserved me so long and blessed me so abundantly! If, as is believed, one person dies every second, then since I was born, two billion, five hundred and thirty-four million, two hundred and eight thousand fellow mortals have gone to their eternal estate. Alas! how few of them have I helped to secure a blessed immortality!"

Six months after this he traced the last words that were ever written in the little memorandum book — a series of quotations: —

FOR MY BREAST IN THE COFFIN.

"By the grace of God I am what I am."

"Into thy hand I commit my spirit."

"Thou hast redeemed me, O Lord God of truth."

"Hallelujah 't is done. I believe in the Son,
I am saved by the blood of the crucified one!"

"Jesus alone can help. Jesus is mine.
Farewell mortality. Jesus is mine.
Welcome eternity. Jesus is mine."

"To lay down my burden at Jesus' feet,
And cease from my toiling and laboring, is sweet."

"I wish the above printed or written very legibly and laid on my shroud as I lie in a very plain, cheap coffin."

He drew the attention of his daughter to this written desire of his and said: "I wish it to be my last sermon." A month later the sermon was preached as he had wished, for the gate had opened and he had passed triumphantly through it.

"There was no marked disease," writes Dr. Gulick, who with his wife was with him at the time; "no pain, only weakness; but he said he thought his feelings indicated a 'breaking up of the old shell.' He suffered little save as weakness is suffering. And though he steadily failed, he was so comfortable that neither he nor we could realize he was so near his end. At three o'clock Saturday afternoon he rose with assistance and sat in his easychair. In doing so he nearly fainted away; and as he recovered from the swoon he spoke of the 'Sun of Righteousness, his only joy and hope,' which he doubtless intended as his last testimonial to the Lord in whom he trusted.

"At seven in the evening he folded his hands upon his breast and a few moments later was sinking in death. He simply stepped across the rill and was gone. His life was finished, his work was done, his words all said.

"On Monday we laid his body to rest in the cemetery of the Foreign Concession under the evergreen pines, near the shores of the Pacific whose billows he daily saw for fifty years, and in whose people, first on the Hawaiian Islands, and then in Japan, he for half a century took such continued interest. And standing about the grave where he rested we sang : —

> 'Asleep in Jesus! Oh, how sweet
> To be for such a slumber meet,
> With holy confidence to sing
> That death hath lost its venomed sting.'"

After that, the other world seemed to overlap the bounds of Kobé. And dear grandmother waited for the call that should take her into it. Since childhood she had dreaded the physical part of dying. But after her husband left her, the fear of it was gone. Being alone one day, she was heard to clap her hands, and when they asked her about it she said she did it because she was so very happy; that at last her prayers were answered, for now she had no fear of death at all.

As a result her thoughts were often on the other side. Most of her friends were there, she said. And with paper and pencil and trembling fingers she made a list one day of those she hoped to recognize when she should join them.

Six years seemed long to wait, while she grew more feeble every day. But at last the angels and the final summons seemed very near. She was ill. She heard faint music in the distance, and as she listened, she hoped it came from heaven, but the delicate, quaint humor of her thinking did not leave her even then. She whispered to her daughter that she should not believe it was the angels unless they sang a little louder. After that, one day, a whispered prayer of hers was overheard. "Dear Jesus," the sweet old lady prayed, "please send the angels to carry me home. I am so tired."

In 1883 her prayer was answered, for the angels came very quietly and carried her with them to heaven.

CHAPTER XXVIII.

BIBLE WORK.

THOUGH special grants of money had already been made by the American Bible Society for work in Japan, still the Society had no personal organizing agent there till Dr. Gulick arrived. In China, however, the same Society had been active for years and had appropriated something like $220,000 to the needs of that country between 1833 and 1876. Hence, conditions in the two empires were not the same.

"In Japan," writes Dr. Gulick, "everything is initiatory. Here it will be safe for me to be radical, progressive. In China, Bible affairs are already in deep ruts and I must be very careful and conservative and fortified by precedents."

He realized that there was danger of a little friction in the work he had been set to do; and that this danger lay in the sensitiveness of corporations no less than of individuals. He feared lest some one should feel that past efforts were not appreciated because new methods were adopted, lest the old should feel crowded out by the new.

Bearing this in mind, his effort was to avoid the

infliction of any pain to sensitive souls by the way he organized his work and gradually set the wheels within the wheels to moving. As a result his relation to societies and individuals was cordial from the beginning and increasingly satisfactory to him as time passed by.

In its primary divisions the work of the Bible Society covered the three departments of translation, publication, and distribution of the Scriptures. The Society itself stood as a great auxiliary to every denomination of Protestant American missionaries in China and Japan. When necessary, it paid the salaries of those missionaries who devoted themselves exclusively to Bible translation. It paid for the publication of these translations and supplied each American mission station with all that was desired of the whole or of special parts of the Bible.[1]

These missionaries were, in turn, the natural centers of circulation. There was great dissimilarity in the methods they adopted. Some gave the Bible to all who would accept it; some charged a few cents for it, while others decided in each case as to the wisest course. Furthermore, some stations were exact and some were inexact in their annual reports to the Bible Society, and some sent no reports at all.

[1] English and Scotch Bible Societies did the same work for the representatives of their countries.

It had, indeed, been difficult to require reports, or uniformity of action in the past. But now it was needed. And in this effort after reorganization, in this replacing of chaos by method, there was satisfaction for most, though a few felt hampered by it.

The requirement was nevertheless imperative, and Dr. Gulick moved quietly on with what he had to do. He sent to each missionary catalogues of the Bible as printed in different forms and sections with the prices attached, with blanks also for annual book and cash reports, and simple directions for their use. It was for him to gather into one pair of hands the many strands which connected the American missions in Japan and China with the American Bible Society in America.

Through the cordial support of Dr. Gilman, the Secretary of the Bible Society, and the hearty coöperation of the missionaries this was accomplished. It was soon possible to begin the work of rapidly increasing the circulation of the Bible in the two empires. Everything favored this movement in Japan. In the first place, Dr. Gulick himself was stationed there, his home being in Yokohama. In the second place, the Japanese were just entering that era of national excitement when everything foreign was welcome to them. In a sense, therefore, the Bible also shared their curiosity. This fact may explain, in part, the phenomenal sales made in 1880. A foreign colporter was the immediate agent, while his Bible carriage drawn by a horse, his Bible cart drawn by a man, his magic lantern and his singing were his instruments. For a season hundreds of copies were sold each day.

"Mr. Goble has been in Tokio this week," writes Dr. Gulick, "selling Scriptures from our new and beautiful Bible handcart at an average of over five hundred portions a day!!! The cart sold during its first few days in Tokio over three thousand portions. A new era has dawned in Bible work for Japan." At the same time he adds: "The proprietors of eighteen little steamers plying on the rivers about Tokio have accepted copies of the New Testament which are kept in the cabins for the use of passengers."

Copies were also allowed in railway waiting rooms. Indeed, it appears that during 1880, after the completion of the translation of the New Testament, "We printed and distributed more Scriptures than had been printed and distributed during all the previous years of Bible work in Japan — over eleven million pages printed, and over ten million sold."

"We now have a Bible house in Yokohama," he says, "built for our use and rented for a term of years. And this Bible house of ours is a grand success, one of the successes of my life."

In 1881 business is reported as having "increased about fourfold in six months." The beginning of these enterprises had required more thought and labor than can easily be comprehended without full exposition of the details.

"There is little to tell about myself," he wrote at the close of 1878. "I have been staggering under heavy burdens of work which have almost crushed me, so that my health threatened to give way altogether, but I am pulling through.

"I am gradually getting my heterogeneous and scattered work into shape and can begin to see daylight; that is, to see a possible execution of my duties as Bible agent. I now address myself with new vigor to my work. There is ample field for enlargement. No pent-up Utica!"

This plan for enlargement was so seriously followed, and the movement in each country was so rapid during the first five years of his connection with it, that by 1881 the Bible Society concurred with him in the judgment that his field should be divided.

He was allowed to choose the larger country. After that his work was in China and his home in Shanghai.

For China this was a happy arrangement, for in whichever country he had previously spent his time there the progress had been most rapid. It was as if the engineer were present with a strong hand upon the throttle of his engine. He knew how to add steam to the movement, and he knew how fast it was safe to let the engine go. Some notion of this work in China may be gathered from the statement of a few facts about it.

The heaviest part of Bible translation had already been done. The Bible as a whole, as New Testament and Old Testament, as separate gospels and epistles, was published in seven different languages, and catalogued as ninety-one different volumes. In China, therefore, the burden of effort was to provide the straightest channels through which to reach three hundred million people with these translations.

For Dr. Gulick native and foreign colporters were these channels. When he first went to China but five natives were thus employed for the whole of the north and middle region. But by 1884 forty-eight Chinese and nine foreign men were employed by him for practically the same service. And by 1886 his figures proved that five sixths of his whole work of circulation was done by these Christian men, and that two thirds of this was through the Chinese themselves. In many cases these colporters were the pioneers of the missionary. And for the sake of helping them Dr. Gulick not infrequently accompanied a foreign colporter on an extended tour into the heart of China.

These journeys were the most intimate kind of introduction to the traveling facilities of the country. For six hundred miles sometimes he steamed up the Yang-tse-Kiang River in a large paddle-wheel steamer.

"As we look along the river on which a mighty commerce comes and goes," he says, "it is mortifying to find so conspicuous among river steamers and ocean steamships, gallant sail vessels and clumsy junks, also those unsightly covered hulks in which the opium of English India is stowed, because the Chinese will not allow its being otherwise than surreptitiously kept on Chinese soil." [1]

At other times he was on a junk or a flat-bottomed house boat. Instead of steam there would now be a sail or the current to help them, or men with long poles to propel, or men upon the shore with tow-line fastened to the mast to draw them along. All this was the method upon the great rivers and upon the canals which cover central China as railroads lace New England.

By land there were horses and donkeys and springless carts, and palanquins with porters, and jinrikishas

---

[1] "How affecting," he says, "to find the stolid Chinaman in his government relations steadily refusing any complicity with this destroying item of commerce. And how sad to know that opium is forced upon China by nominally Christian guns and bayonets. God speed the day when truly Christian England, by continued appeals to its Bible-educated conscience, shall have raised such a sentiment as to sweep this trade, so far as enactments can do it, from both land and sea."

drawn by men and mule litters. But most amusing of all were the wheelbarrows, with a donkey to draw them and a sail to help the donkey along. Yet, whether the methods were one or many, whether the conveyances were few or numberless, the progress was always slow. Why, indeed, hasten in a country whose authentic history outdates the flood and whose future has the whole of time before it!

During these journeys all kinds of fair weather and dreadful tempests overtook them, and every sort of physical discomfort. At the mouth of the Peiho River Dr. Gulick once wrote: "It is now seventy-two hours that we have lain here — stranded and waiting for the tide to rise."

A few months later on the same river and for an opposite reason there was cause for delay quite as great and far more serious.

"We are to-day sailing over ricefields and cornpatches, and over the tops of houses on our way back to Kiukiang. The bund is under water and the streets are traversed with boats. One of the great overflows of this great land and these mighty waters. We travel the streets in boats, and kingfishers dart down upon the fish among the flowerbeds of the garden." With these floods there also came terrible famine for millions of people. "Five or six million who have starved to death," he says, "but who, after a little, will hardly be missed, for lives and suffering are superabundant already and always in China."

Beginning his missionary life with the consecration of Luther he carried it on like Paul. In journeyings oft, in storms by sea and by land, in comfort and discomfort, with friends sometimes, in loneliness often, but rejoicing always that the privilege was still given him of helping to carry the gospel to those who have it not.

Being gray at fifty-two, the Chinese paid him a certain sort of deference, though the expression of it was sometimes novel. They asked him whether he were eighty or ninety years old, and distinguishing him from others whom they called "Foreign Devils," they called him the "Old Devil." But it may be, as he himself said, "The element of oldness probably balanced somewhat the disadvantage of being a foreign devil!" In any case they were more ready to take foreign books from the older than from the younger man. There was certainly an advantage in gray hairs in this land, where instinctive honor is paid to aged people.

In journeying as he did, and in studying the movement of the nation, he was increasingly impressed by the magnitude of the work and by the power which China seemed to hold as a mighty storage battery of human force which should yet be drawn upon.

"It is thirty years this fall," he writes, "since we left Boston for Micronesia, but it looks to me as if I had just entered my life's great work. It is a great privilege to be here to have a part; and China moves! A new nation is being born, and what it will be we tremble to think. I pity the soul that turns away with a want of interest in China."

"It seems to me that this is the grandest mission field in the world. I don't understand the reluctance and fear of many young people."

"China is circling toward a maelstrom, and now is the time to work for her. Ten years hence the relations of things will be changed and then Congregationalism will probably come puffing and blowing into the field, too late to take its proper place."

"China will be a mighty nation long after America and Japan have 'progressed' into oblivion."

Thus from the smallness of Micronesia Dr. Gulick had moved step by step to the largeness of the Orient. There were millions now for the hundreds then; but the spirit that moved him remained the same. It still led him to unsparing devotion of himself even in lines of effort that were wholly uncongenial to him.

In China extensive bookkeeping was the uncongenial duty. The enlargement of the work there was so rapid that the expenditure of the Bible Society in that country alone soon reached the large sum of twenty-five thousand dollars a year. This meant mathematics in earnest. And in this connection it is interesting to know that when Dr. Gulick was a small boy of five no one could confuse him on the multiplication table under the twelve-times-twelve, but that through the whole of his later life figures in any shape were a weariness to him. No pleasure in the work itself ever led him to undertake anything mathematical. Now, however, the necessity had come to him as a duty. In serious earnest he therefore studied bookkeeping as he had never studied it before, and lay awake at night over the peculiar difficulties which accompanied the inevitable complexity of his book accounts.

Of necessity these accounts were kept with each separate denomination of Americans in China; with many of the two hundred and eighty individual members of these denominations; with forty-seven colporters; with publishing houses, and with various other organizations and individuals who were more or less directly connected with Bible Society moneys; and though before many months he mastered the science of bookkeeping and narrowed it down to a very fine point of exactness, yet he never enjoyed it. It was always drudgery to him and he cried out against it sometimes, even as he had cried out against cooking in Micronesia years before.

"I was not cut out for a bookkeeper!" he exclaims. "Why should we be put to work for which we have no fitness?"

"I am at work every evening till ten and eleven o'clock, and last night till half-past one at my books."

"I have closed up my 1885 accounts without any assistance, and yesterday the auditors examined and approved them. I consider it quite a feat to foot up a balance sheet involving over twenty thousand dollars without an error of one cent in the most scientific methods of double entry!"

"Is it not a singular ordering that gives me, who have no aptitude for figures, the bookkeeping incident to an expenditure of twenty-five thousand dollars? Something not well arranged somewhere; but as it is given me to do, I put my strength into it."

This faithfulness was in harmony with the full investment of himself which he had made and there were rapid returns. Through increased organization and enlargement of his agencies the pages of the Bible were finding their way into many parts of previously unreached, conservative China. From a circulation of 74,800 volumes in 1878, the number distributed every year rose by jumps until, during 1887, there was an actual distribution through the American Bible Society alone of 252,875 copies. The significance of these figures was emphasized in

1891, when a successor in the work, Dr. Wheeler, wrote of Dr. Gulick: —

"I find everywhere traces of his master hand in the formation and shaping of the operations of the American Bible Society in these ends of the earth."

CHAPTER XXIX.

OVERWORK.

IN addition to the pressure of Bible work, Dr. Gulick was constantly tempted to assume other responsibilities. The strongest of these temptations came with the frequent invitation to preach in English. In 1880, while yet in Japan, he says: —

"My powers have been taxed to the utmost in meeting the demands of my agency alone. And besides this, I have preached twice almost every Sabbath of the year to the Union Church of Yokohama,[1] and done what little I could of pastoral work. Consequently this has been a busy year. And now, the more I rest, the more I want to."

But having once started in the line of overwork, it was increasingly difficult to secure release from it. For, after Japan, there was China. And from the Union Church of Yokohama, how refuse the urgency of the other union church, in the still more enterprising city of Shanghai?[2] There again he therefore

---

[1] The first thousand dollars paid toward the erection of this first Protestant church in Japan was given by the Christians in Hawaii.

[2] He thus pictures the city: "Just outside and to the north of the mediæval city, along the low bank and the muddy, sluggish river, is

preached. His supply of the pulpit was irregular at first, but it resulted in a continuous pastorate of the church from 1887 to 1889. And in Shanghai, as in Yokohama, the audience increased in size as he remained connected with it.

The building itself was new and had cost thirty-five thousand dollars. It seated three hundred people, and numbered among its members eleven different denominations.

"Of necessity, there is no very compact organization," Dr. Gulick says, "the machinery of church life being left at a minimum for the sake of avoiding every possibility of friction. But no church in any part of the world is more united in the matters on which it unites."

It was a pleasure to minister to such an organization. And yet the men and women who listened to him every Sabbath little realized how much this preaching signified to their pastor himself. Through it he entered the citadel of his lifelong enthusiasm, the "castle in Spain" which he had dreamed about in his boyhood, and the gleaming of whose towers had

---

the foreign city of Shanghai, resplendent with banks, hotels, and commercial houses. Its streets are wide and smooth as the most perfect macadam can make them; and they overflow with life: — a vast portion of it being the stalwart, almond-eyed, flowing-robed, and shrewdly industrious Celestial. But the vitalizing element of it is the short-haired, unpicturesquely clothed, yet tremendously energetic European, mainly English."

been his inspiration ever since. His thought was that in preaching every Sabbath he would gain enough mental reinvigoration to compensate him for the nervous force expended.[1]

The audience itself was not large, but it was thoughtful and appreciative. It included business men of such energy that they had gone halfway round the world to make their fortune; sea captains, officers, and crew, who never went to church from sense of duty; missionaries, also, and teachers who had practically expatriated themselves for the sake of China. Besides these, there was the literary tramp, and the ministerial tramp, and the wealthy tramp; all of whom, either in the pursuit of fame, or to satisfy a morbid curiosity to see "the heathen," or to spend superfluous time and money, formed a restless current of eager humanity moving round the world together.

In addition to his preaching, there was sometimes a lecture, or an address, or a temperance talk to be given. Of one of these, he writes: "A daily paper calls it 'a witty speech,' the other says it was 'a spirited address,' from which you will gather about what it was."

The evident brightness of the address but points

---

[1] In deciding the matter he wrote: "If I can serve the church and the Bible Society, I may think of it; otherwise, I give up the church."

his cheerful mental condition during these years. It is easy, indeed, to recognize the satisfaction he felt in having, as he says, "found his niche." He was working, it is true, as never before in his life. Yet the work itself was a delight to him. He was touching many people. His thoughts were drawn away from himself. For years now introspective musings had been laid aside, and the more normal attitude of religious life had taken its place.

Those were happy years in China, yet they were overcrowded. First there was his Bible work. Then there was the burning of nervous force in preaching, and besides was the tax which came in 1885, when he consented to be the literary editor of The Chinese Recorder. This was a magazine of high literary grade, printed in the English language in Shanghai. It was issued once in two months. Later yet, but at the same time that he carried all his other duties, Dr. Gulick was chosen business editor of The Chinese Medical Journal, a quarterly magazine. And though he groaned somewhat in protest he did not refuse the position.

The truth is that words of encouragement and appreciation always acted upon him as a tonic, and that, at this time, so many kind and cordial remarks were made to him about the methods of his work, and the help he was to others, that a certain sort of strength came with them which he failed to recognize as fictitious. He was simply stimulated to yet larger effort.

"I enjoy preaching more, I think, than ever," he writes, "for the church is very cordial and it is pleasant work."

"Within a few weeks I have received more expressions of appreciation than in all my life before. It is very pleasant."

"I am impressed with the delights of my present form of work. Never before have I had everything so satisfactory. It is of the Lord."

"I seem to myself to have taken a new lease of life. New vistas of pleasure and usefulness are opening before me."

"I am beginning to receive commendations from many parties here about The Recorder. The fact is, it puts me on a vantage ground for Bible work such as nothing else could give me. It is as The Kuokoa was to me on the Hawaiian Islands in my work as Secretary."

"I am receiving many commendations and the circulation is going up steadily."

"I am almost too nicely fixed in almost every way — in my business and in my home. I wonder how long it will last! I have a hope and a feeling that I am to be more permanent in the present work than I have been in any other, and that I have made my last great change in life's activities."[1]

Projected as pebbles into the hurrying current of this life were various other events that produced more or less disturbance of the surface. Of least importance, perhaps, was the honorary degree of D.D. conferred upon him by Knox College. This drew bright comments from his pen as he begged his friends not to use it.

"Please do not address me as D.D.," he writes to one. "The semi-lunar fardels are well enough, but it would be far better if they could be arranged symmetrically, one before and one after the name. To put them both after it acts something like a leaden sinker to a fish-line."

And to another: "It is nothing to be specially jubilant over. They did not know me or they would not have done it. It was a sort of accident. I must take it as Dr. Thompson, of Roxbury, says Dr. Anderson took his D.D., knowing that, like the rain from heaven, they fall on the just and on the unjust. Please address me as heretofore."

Clearly enough, titles of honor meant little. But Dr. and Mrs. Gulick felt that honor itself had come to

---

[1] During the summer of 1883 he had visited America, joining his wife, who had previously returned for her health. Both parents were present at the graduation of their sons Sidney and Edward from Dartmouth College.

them when two of their children turned to foreign missionary work. This occurred in 1887. A daughter with her husband [1] then went to Japan via San Francisco, while a son [2] and his wife also joined the same mission of the American Board, reaching it via Europe and China. It was a great day for the home in Shanghai when the parents there waited to welcome their oldest son and his young wife. "We are in a high state of excitement for two such old people," wrote Dr. Gulick to his brother. "Thank God and rejoice with us." On the twenty-second of December, 1887, a very brief note was hurried through the mail.

"Dear Orramel. They have come. HALSEY."

Other pebbles that created small eddies for a season were the different calls that came to him. One begged him to join the Chinese mission work as a regular physician. Another wished him to accept the presidency of a college in China. Still another asked for the use of his name as director of a university proposed for Shanghai.

But moving him most was an earnest call from the Hawaiian Evangelical Association, emphasized by request from the American Board and by urgent personal letters from his friends on Hawaii, that he return to his old position as Secretary of the Hawaiian Board.

[1] Rev. Cyrus A. Clark.
[2] Rev. Sidney L. Gulick.

This call gratified him more than any other that ever came to him. "You cannot know how moved I am in this matter," he writes. "Did I suppose that I were indispensable to the good cause among you, I should return as soon as possible."

But because the Bible Society now had prior claim upon him, and because he seemed peculiarly adapted to his work in China, he thought it would not be right to accept the invitation. It was hard to decide against it, for he loved Hawaii as tenderly now as in his earlier years. His best judgment guided him, however, and he remained where he was. "My last opportunity of spending my remaining days among the friends of younger years thus passes," he says. "My heart is moved."

There was yet another call for immediate help which Dr. Gulick answered in the affirmative without a moment's hesitation. This came from his old fellow worker, Mr. Doane, in Micronesia.

It appears that, even in 1885, troubles had begun for Micronesia in the counter-claims of Germany and Spain for possession of the microscopic Caroline Islands. These islands were worth something to commerce now, for thirty-five years of American Christianity had borne their legitimate fruit. To large extent, heathenism had given place to Christianity, and Ponape herself was sending foreign missionaries to the more distant and degraded Mortlock Islands.

The transformation was so complete that it was no more strange than it was unjustifiable that two great Christian powers on the other side of the world, in their wish to own the beautiful, helpless islands, should have been willing to rob them of their manhood: two powers, which since the beginning had never, by the slightest word or act, helped them to secure their civilization. The question of right was submitted to the Pope for decision. "And thus a Christian minister decides which of two thieves shall have the property they have stolen!" is the indignant comment which Dr. Gulick made.

In March, 1887, the end came to Ponapean independence. A Spanish gunboat arrived with "governor, troops, convicts, and Capuchin monks."

"The natives take it quietly but sorrowfully," writes Mr. Doane. "I advise the truest submission. It is our only safety. And I am happy to say they obey."

After that, events moved rapidly until, on the thirteenth of April, the Spanish governor imprisoned Mr. Doane on a series of false charges; kept him a prisoner on his man-of-war in Ponapean waters for three months, and finally deported him two thousand miles to Manila "for trial," as he said. Arriving there, Mr. Doane was not prevented from mailing his letters. Dr. Gulick was filled with indignation when he read them. With characteristic energy, however, he went at once to the Consul General of the United States to China; wrote to Rear Admiral Ralph Chandler, commanding the Asiatic Squadron; vigorously reviewed the case for him, and showed to him the interest America necessarily had in her American citizens on Ponape.

"It is not for me to say," he wrote, "what assistance may be rendered Mr. Doane by your department of authority, but I should evidently be derelict in my duty to the United States government, no less than to you and to my friend Mr. Doane, and to the interests of the missionary society with which he is connected, did I not give you the information which, probably, I alone possess in all this region, and which I should hope might seem to you to render it advisable that a United States vessel of war be ordered with dispatch to Manila."

Further than this, he sent three hundred dollars to Mr. Doane at once by telegram, and in writing to him urged that he have " as clear and full a written statement of the case as possible — statements that will be available in America and Spain."

"You must plan to come up to China," he adds, "and make us a good long visit; it will do us good."

Happily the authorities in Manila were not willing

to support the extreme policy of the Catholic governor of Ponape; and without time for a visit to Shanghai, Mr. Doane was returned to Ponape.[1]

Official word soon came from mission societies in America thanking Dr. Gulick for the promptness of his action. But the truth is, that, in behalf of his own love for Micronesia, he could not have done less than he did. For, until he passed away, the most real and central point of his life seems to have been those early years on Ponape. And references to them are constant through all that he wrote.

Once in voyaging he passed an atoll. "And I could not but ascend the rigging of the mainmast," he says, " to look down as I often did in Micronesian waters upon the long line of cocoanut and pandanus, the straggling reef, the outer line of sand, the inner peaceful lagoon and the few huts on the outer reef. None of my fellow passengers knew, or could have appreciated had they known, the thoughts that surged

---

[1] In 1894, after the annual return of the Morning Star to Honolulu, Rev. O. H. Gulick thus reports the latest news from Ponape: "King Paul of the Matalanim tribe is a Christian apostle of power in his tribe. He urges his people to serve the Prince of Peace with all their heart, and to fight the Spanish invader with all their might. That is the tribe in which Halsey and Louise lived when I visited them in 1857, thirty-seven years ago! Twice in bloody battle have the Spaniards been driven defeated from the bounds of this plucky little tribe, whose members, under the lead of their God-fearing King Paul, are determined to sell their lives dear, and their liberties dearer than their lives. For five long years this valiant tribe has held the Spaniard at bay. God bless them and help them ever to stand to their purpose."

within me. I often wonder why, with such a commencement to our missionary life, we have led such lives as we have. Were we not adapted, or were we not worthy?

"And yet my prevailing feeling is that of thankfulness that, as we could not return to those silent seas, we have been permitted to have some part in foreign missionary work in foreign lands. But how little missionary fruitage compared with what we had hoped, and with what we should have had, had we continued in Micronesia! But we only 'followed on.'"

Dr. Gulick seemed still to be following on. Yet it is doubtless true that editorship and preaching added to the great work which he did as agent of the Bible Society for the whole of China, with Siam finally added to it, were shortening his days. But who questions what his choice would have been? — the shorter life with the delight of preaching and writing crowded into it, or the weary adding of figures and the practice of double entry carried on through the unillumined length of a few added years.

Still, whether he would have chosen it or not, the fact remains that the zeal for work which was his master was driving him rapidly toward a master yet more inexorable, and that from him there would soon be no escape. Dr. Gulick himself did not realize how swift this movement was. For us, however, various passages make distinct prophecy.

1882. "I am beginning to find that my headaches are ceasing to yield to the medicines I have been accustomed to use."

1883. "I am so pressed I hardly have a minute to breathe save in the evening sometimes, when I am tired out."

"I am too tired to read even, I can only write! Pretty far gone you see!"

"On the tenth I was taken down with the most serious attack of spasmodic asthma I ever experienced. It had been coming on for eighteen hours. At last, I left my office, took to my lounge, sent for the doctor, and did not stir from my sitting position for forty-eight hours. I am left very weak and sore."

1884. "How we whirl! . . . I am hard at work writing. I suppose when I have ceased to write my life will end! . . . I spent a part of last night in bed; the first time in ten or more nights because of asthma. . . . I am troubled with asthma so much that I find it most convenient not to go to bed, but to sleep on the lounge, which I do very comfortably. . . . I am under a tearing headache. I can hardly see my pen."

1885. "I am, after two days, slowly recovering from one of the most terrific headaches I ever had.

My head very nearly failed me notwithstanding all the medicines I took — one hundred and twenty-five grains of bromide of potassia and forty grains of hydrochloral in five hours! . . . The Recorder, my annual accounts and reports, my speech for resigning the Presidency of the Evangelical Alliance on the first day of the week of prayer, all make me very busy. . . . What with my office business, my Recorder, and my lecture on the Caroline Islands, I am busy enough."

1886. "I am rushing every moment and shall be loth to get back into the heavy strain of the last two years. Indeed, it does not seem to me that I ought to subject myself to such a strain again. . . . Fifty-eight years old! Hard at work all day with not a leisure moment till this evening. No time for excitement. . . . I never have done more than during the past year. Up till half-past one preparing sermon because there had been no time before."

1887. "I have had the busiest year of my life. I have put on all steam so as not to let any of the interests suffer, and now that all is getting along so satisfactorily I shall take matters less nervously though I shall still be busy."

1888. "I have delivered a lecture on recent discoveries in the Holy Land this week, and preached two sermons last Sabbath and am to preach two next Sabbath."

"My digestive system is giving way."

"I am taking business quite easily, though most people would think themselves overpressed with what I am still doing."

"Pray for me that these closing years, this last stage of my life's work may be usefully spent — spent in a way and with results that may finally justify my having entered this work."

"I should enjoy several months of entire relaxation."

"A Happy New Year to you all! The wish is a heartless sort of thing, and I seldom repeat the formula without a chill. And soon the chill will be in death. But how little it will matter save to ourselves!"

"God bless you all, and grant that we may find one another out after death."

"How soon may it be before we shall be measuring the lapse of eternity rather than time; and who of us knows what that means?"

CHAPTER XXX.

THE END.

THERE was no radical lessening of the work he did and no marked increase of suffering through headache and asthma until the early part of 1889. Then, without any announcement of it, the crisis of his life of overwork reached him suddenly. It showed itself first in a sense of utter prostration and weariness. Absolute rest was essential. This involved at least a temporary absence from China. Japan was the nearest point and they went to their children in Kumamoto. Here his prostration was so extreme that for days death seemed imminent.

He rallied somewhat, but the best of medical aid was imperative, and once more Dr. and Mrs. Gulick crossed the Pacific together — the last time that he ever sailed upon the ocean.

The headache of past years came to him now in spasms: "tempests of pain" he called them. But to those who were with him the pain seemed agony, for he grew white even to the lips at such times and could not speak.

When they reached San Francisco, there had already

come to him the feebler step of old age and the uncertain walk. Weary months followed. Physicians were full of kindness and they helped him for a season. Sanitarium life in California and New York seemed to give temporary aid, while the unwearied devotion of his wife was the anchor which held him most firmly to life. On the whole, however, those slow months from 1889 to 1891 were an inclined plane down which he was steadily moving. By the first of 1891 the end seemed very near. There was such weakness that even his pain was conquered by it. For many weeks he did not even touch his pen.

He was in New York city again, and skillful physicians there were again doing all they could to help him. Yet no man, however gifted in the art of healing, can create new wheels for the machinery of life when the old ones have passed all hope of repairing. At best he can only hope to add a few revolutions to the halting movement. And so the worn-out man tarried for a while in this city from which, forty years before, he had looked out with eager expectation on all that life might bring to him. He was back again in it with all that life had brought to him — with all that was left of life!

At fourteen he had been older than his years. And though in the number of them he was now only sixty-two, still in the measure of what he had accomplished, in his crowded life of thought, in the height and depth and intensity of his varied experiences, he was older than sixty-two by many years — a shock of corn fully ripe. His hair was white, his face was thin, while his form, from the energy and the strength of a vigorous prime, had within two years taken on the shrunken outlines of an aged man. Weakness was added to weakness, and I who am his daughter had gone to help our mother for a season in her care of him. No one understood his need quite so well as she did, so he told us, but for her sake he gently acquiesced when others tried to help him.

It was Sabbath morning, and the sound of chimes in the distance and the quiet of the street brought a touch of holiness even to the metropolis. For the sake of change in position I had raised our father in his bed with many pillows. Then I stood behind him, and while I stroked his head we talked a little very quietly. It was not often that he spoke of death; more often, indeed, he spoke of plans to be carried out when he should be stronger, and very often of his hope to visit Hawaii once more. For " those islands seem more like home to me," he said, " than any place on earth." But for several days he had questioned its possibility.

" If there is n't a change pretty soon," he said, " I think there never will be. I am growing very weak."

Once or twice he had also said: "I think we'll have to give it up, Fanny. It's a pretty hard pull, and two years of it. Don't you think I have had a hard time?"

"O father," I would answer, "if any of us could bear it for you, how gladly we would do it!"

On this Sabbath we had been talking about studies and reading, and father said: "Fanny, try to avoid the mistake I have made. Emphasize the spiritual part of your life. My danger has always been my temptation to pay most attention to the intellectual. But the spiritual must not be neglected. It cannot grow if neglected." Then, after a pause, he added: "You will remember this when I am gone, will you not? Remember this is my dying message to you all."

The promise made was very solemn. And standing as I did he could not see my tears, but I told him that he must not leave us yet, that all his past life had been but preparation for what he yet would do. He only answered: "I am not sure. I am growing weaker every day."

After that he spoke of some one who had recently died. And in my great desire to hear him testify about it I almost whispered my abrupt question: "Father, do you wholly believe in a personal immortality?"

And he answered instantly, in a voice that had a note of triumph in it: "I believe it wholly."

How blessed the peace of dying in this great assurance! And our father had it.

For the sake of being nearer to his children [1] the last weeks of his life were spent in Springfield, Massachusetts, and they were very peaceful weeks. No physical suffering marked them and no apparent mental unrest. The storm of life, its noise and its confusion lay behind him, and heaven was nearer every day.

"What do you think about most of the time, Halsey?" his wife asked one day.

"Nothing," he answered. "I don't seem to have strength enough to think. I just lie here."

Everything gentle and beautiful pleased him, and his eyes brightened always when delicate flowers were sent to him. The mute things, the silent, restful things, were perhaps most in harmony with the quiet harbor which he seemed to have entered even now. Many times when he could not sleep at night he found comfort in the gentle singing of his wife, and in the Psalms and Bible chapters, which at his request she recited to him.

On the eighth of April, 1891, at one o'clock in the afternoon, the greater peace came to him. There was

---

[1] Rev. Edward Leeds Gulick was at the time pastor of the Congregational church of Groton, Massachusetts. Luther Halsey Gulick, Jr., M.D., was the director of the gymnasium department of the Y. M. C. A. Training School located in Springfield. Pierre Johnson Gulick, the youngest son, was also in Springfield preparing for college.

DR. AND MRS. GULICK.

no moment of warning nor time for parting words. His breath simply fluttered for a moment and then was gone. The gate had opened noiselessly, and one more brave soul had joined " the choir invisible whose music is the gladness of the world."

Two days later the precious earthly part of him was laid to rest under the whispering pine trees of the Springfield cemetery. A partially smoothed block of gray granite marks the spot, and on it the history of his life is very simply told.

LUTHER HALSEY GULICK.

BORN, HONOLULU, HAWAII, 1828.
DIED, SPRINGFIELD, 1891.

FOR FORTY YEARS A FOREIGN MISSIONARY.

CHAPTER XXXI.

THE LAST DAYS OF MRS. GULICK.

SINCE the preceding chapters were written, Mrs. Gulick too has passed away. It seems fitting, therefore, that some record of the closing of her beautiful life should bring this volume to a close.

From Springfield she returned to Japan to join her children in their mission work. Four other children were in the United States; and filial love, therefore, claimed her alike for America and Japan. But the devotion of her life drew her to what seemed to her the more needy land. Her children themselves no longer required her care. "And I am afraid," she said, "that I am not very brave, not brave enough to be willing to stay in America and add one more to the multitude of idle Christians."

The decision was accordingly made. She was to sail from Vancouver during the summer of 1891. But, before she went, we again visited the cemetery in Springfield together.

It was at sunset; and as we walked the heated street, flying clouds of dust sometimes almost blinded us. But as the bee wings its straight course to the hive, its home, so our mother went straight and swift through the lonely place, toward the spot where her husband lay.

Once more she was near to him, and the world was forgotten. She remembered only the hours by day and by night when her singing had soothed him. So now, in the twilight among the pine trees, while he lay beneath in dreamless sleep, she sang for the last time near him. Her voice sometimes quavered and almost failed, but her soul believed the words she sang.

> "Asleep in Jesus! blessed sleep!
> From which none ever wake to weep;
> A calm and undisturbed repose,
> Unbroken by the last of foes.
>
> Asleep in Jesus! peaceful rest;
> Whose waking is supremely blest;
> No fear, no woe shall dim that hour
> Which manifests the Saviour's power.
>
> Asleep in Jesus! oh, for me
> May such a blissful refuge be!
> Securely shall my ashes lie,
> And wait the summons from on high."

Even the crickets were silent as she sang, and the angels drew near and comforted her. So it seemed, for her voice grew a little stronger, and there was growing peace. Then she almost whispered: "How he loved to hear me sing! He said it comforted him.

Oh, why should I allow myself to suffer so? It is well with him I know. All his weakness and suffering ended! Heaven for him now, and I shall join him soon. Oh, my dear one! my dear one! it will be heaven next time we meet!"

Six weeks later she had reached Japan.

To a large extent the succeeding two and a half years of her life were spent in the home of her daughter, Mrs. Clark. This home was in Miyazaki, in the province of Hiuga. And in this remote, interior town, where no other foreigners lived, but where the natives were willing to listen, Mrs. Gulick devoted her time, her thought, and her prayers, by day and by night, to the instruction of the people. Especially did she work among the women and the children. With a trained Japanese girl whom she taught, she made extended tours among the towns of the neighborhood; and, speaking through her interpreter, she held the attention and won the hearts of the people.

The pressing thought of her life was that opportunity was still given to her, and that souls about her were dying with no knowledge of Christ.

In the midst of busy activity illness came to her suddenly, accompanied by terrible physical suffering. Her son Sidney was summoned by telegraph. It was soon apparent that her only hope of recovery was through a surgical operation. But the Japanese physician had not the needed instruments, and the mission doctor could not at once secure a passport permitting him to come to her. There was, therefore, no alternative. She must, if possible, go to him.

She knew how near death might be, and in speaking about it, said that she "was glad to die if it were the Lord's will, but that there were so many people still unsaved that she had thought she was still to work for them many years."

For the journey she was placed upon a cot-bed, and kindly Japanese jinrikisha men carried her as gently as they could upon their shoulders. All hoped that she might at least reach Kobé, but heaven was nearer to her than Kobé, though they did not know it.

As they approached the town of Takanabe, her pulse grew gradually weaker. Death was very near; and for several miles before they reached the place, both son and daughter walked beside the cot and watched their mother. A sad procession! She was unconscious, but they wanted to be near her through what might prove to be the closing moments of her life. She lived, however, till the town itself was reached, and she was gently laid in the pleasant Japanese room with its soft, white mats. Then, while she was still unconscious, her release came. The mystery of pain was ended and the mystery of peace begun. This was on the fourteenth of June, 1894.

From Takanabe they moved on to Kobé, for the burial of the precious body. Friends were at the landing place to meet them, with the hearse and beautiful flowers; and they went at once from the small steamer to the burial place.

One more grave had been made in the heavy, sandy soil of the foreign cemetery. And here, as near to her little son Ollie as they could place her, with Grandfather and Grandmother Gulick beside her, the brave, worn body was laid to rest. Perhaps her freed spirit was near enough to hear them as they sang of her the words she loved : —

> "Asleep in Jesus! oh, how sweet
> To be for such a slumber meet!
> With holy confidence to sing
> That death has lost its venomed sting."

Ten thousand miles of land and water divide forever all that is mortal of our father and our mother, but, for all time to come, their spirits are united in God.

www.ingramcontent.com/pod-product-compliance
Lightning Source LLC
Chambersburg PA
CBHW030741230426
43667CB00007B/798